Historic ALABAMA BELLS

THOMAS KAUFMANN

Published by The History Press
Charleston, SC
www.historypress.com

Copyright © 2019 by Thomas Kaufmann
All rights reserved

First published 2019

Manufactured in the United States

ISBN 9781467144957

Library of Congress Control Number: 2019947290

Notice: The information in this book is true and complete to the best of our knowledge. It is offered without guarantee on the part of the author or The History Press. The author and The History Press disclaim all liability in connection with the use of this book.

All rights reserved. No part of this book may be reproduced or transmitted in any form whatsoever without prior written permission from the publisher except in the case of brief quotations embodied in critical articles and reviews.

I dedicate this book in honor and memory of my dear father and mother, Andrew Joseph Kaufmann and Jane Lawson Kaufmann, and to my beautiful wife, Ann Marie, and our dear son, Tommy.

Soli Deo Gloria

CONTENTS

Preface 7
Acknowledgements 9
Introduction 13

1. Early Bells of Alabama:
   Territory, Statehood, Frontier and Antebellum 21
2. Paul Revere:
   Revolutionary War Hero, Coppersmith and Bellmaker 40
3. Cast by Paul Revere and Son:
   The First United Methodist Church of Tuscaloosa Bell 44
4. Henry N. Hooper and Company, Boston:
   Successor to Paul Revere and Son, Boston 50
5. Cast by Henry N. Hooper and Company, Boston:
   A Striking Tower Clock and Two Steeple Bells 54
6. William Blake: Master Bell Caster for the Revere Bell Foundry 66
7. Cast by Blake Bell Foundry:
   A Gift from Northern Friends—a Second Steeple Bell 70
8. John Wilbank and the Liberty Bell:
   Bellmaker for Independence Hall and
   the Man Who Saved the Liberty Bell 74
9. Cast by J. Wilbank:
   The Greensboro Presbyterian Church Bell 81
10. The Liberty Bell in Alabama:
    The Genuine Article and the Replica 87

Contents

11. The Church of the Nativity:
    First Bell for the CSA and Second Bell Made of Steel ... 95
12. First Presbyterian Church of Wetumpka:
    Church Bell Offered to the CSA and Turned Down ... 97
13. Saint Paul's Episcopal Church:
    How a False Threat of Smallpox Saved the Town
    and the Bell ... 102
14. Old First Presbyterian Church:
    The Church of the Leaders of Secession ... 107
15. Ramer United Methodist Church:
    A Rare Pre–Civil War Bell ... 115
16. Maplesville Baptist Church:
    A Bell Likely from Old Cahawba and a Civil War Survivor ... 120
17. Abbeville Methodist Church:
    Survived Union General Grierson's April 1865
    Campaign to Eufaula ... 125
18. First Baptist Church, Ripley:
    The Bell that Watched Over the Freedom Riders ... 130
19. Mount Zion AME Zion Church:
    The Tower Bell Comes Home for Civil Rights History ... 137
20. Old Ship AME Zion Church:
    Pulling Hard on the Rope ... 141
21. Brown Chapel AME Church, Selma:
    The Bell that Began the March for Civil Rights ... 144
22. Sixteenth Street Baptist Church:
    Tolling for a National Tragedy ... 149
23. Ever Ringing the Bells of Freedom:
    A Bell for Every Historic Civil Rights Church ... 153

Bibliography ... 159
About the Author ... 160

PREFACE

I arrive at the church in the afternoon, and upon entering the base of the tower, I begin my way up the winding stairs to the balcony level and climb the ladder that leads to the hatch. At the top of the ladder I begin carefully pushing on the hatch, which opens into a void of complete darkness.

I ask the reader, what would your next move be if you were me? The account is from a very recent tower climb, and though each climb is different, there are common denominators—fear, risk, adventure, discovery, danger and adrenaline. Every time I climb a tower, I am nervous. Why? It's always about the unknown. You don't know what's there or what the conditions are like up in a steeple, dome or tower. My years of experience in architecture, construction and historic preservation help me read buildings and structural conditions; the most important rule is safety first, so I don't take unnecessary risks, nor should anyone else. Sometimes I don't climb. It's just not safe. At the same time, when I do climb, the result is most rewarding, and that's one of the reasons for writing this book—to share what I have seen. I'll also share what others have photographed and so kindly shared with me when I was not able to climb. For everyone who so generously contributed to this book, I am most grateful—thank you all!

This book has been seven years in the making, and although it has not been an easy book to write, it has been most enjoyable—especially in making new friends along the way. I tried very hard to be as fair as possible in the categories in terms of representing the different historical periods in the

Preface

best manner possible. In a number of instances, some bells fit into several categories, and a number of bells in the Civil War section were cast in the same year: 1859. I tried very earnestly to call and make arrangements with a number of entities to seek permission to climb but either received no response or was met with difficulty in being granted permission. I'm sure that this book could easily be expanded if some of these issues could be resolved and if I could know with reasonable certainty where more historic bells are, specifically the very towers in which they reside. But that's the great fun of researching these wonderful artifacts—the most special ones are many times in the most unlikely of places.

I hope you will enjoy this book.

Thomas Kaufmann
Montgomery, Alabama
May 15, 2019

ACKNOWLEDGEMENTS

Grateful acknowledgement and appreciation are expressed here to those whose invaluable support, help and assistance made this book possible:

My wife, Ann Marie Kaufmann, and our son, Tommy, for your wonderful love, encouragement and support and for believing in me and this work these past seven years; my brothers, Andy and David; my sister, Kathryn; and Pastor Chris Duncan, Trinity Presbyterian Church, Opelika, for your prayers and encouragement. Paul and Marie Majerick, Ms. Juanita Roberts, Ms. Gail Samuel, Ross Leary, Ms. Catherine Tatum, Susan Henderson, David and Betty Jo Phillips, Sonia Hale, Erica Danylchak, Jonathan Underwood, Johnny Chapman, Veronica Cook, Patty Phillips, Janet Harris, Rogers Hunt, Valerie Lee, James I. Barganier, Dart Davis, Ray Williams, June Patterson, Mrs. Rufus T. Ashe, Julian Butler, Corkey and Brenda Nell, Mike and Nikki Roberts, Neil Goeppinger, Christine Bradshaw, Odessa Berry, Jack Ames, Buddy and Stephanie Smith, Emile Dixon, Ryan Schlesinger, Frank McKinnon, Ray Missildine, Gene Ford, Jason Blythe, Don Blair, Georgia Ann Hudson, Jay Lamar, Dr. Richard K. Dozier, Joyce Hubbard, Daya Irene Taylor and June Pavelec Cutchins.

Acknowledgements

Individuals

Donna Cox Baker—Tuscaloosa, Alabama
Steve Beaird, in memoriam—Montgomery, Alabama
Mr. Philip Burns, in memoriam—Montgomery, Alabama
P. Thomas Carroll, senior scholar, Hudson Mohawk Industrial Gateway Museum—Troy, New York
Dana Chandler, university archivist, Tuskegee University Archives—Tuskegee, Alabama
Clem Clapp, First Baptist Church—Maplesville, Alabama
Mr. Harold Coker, in memoriam—Alexander City, Alabama
Linda Derry, director, and Jonathan Matthews, assistant director, Old Cahawba Archaeological Park—Orrville, Alabama
Bob Dickson, Saint Paul's Episcopal Church—Lowndesboro, Alabama
Lindsay Elliot, Vulcan Park—Birmingham, Alabama
Charles P. Everett IV, Mount Zion AME Zion Church—Montgomery, Alabama
James Fuller, Montgomery County Historical Society—Montgomery, Alabama
Robert Gianini, Liberty Bell Museum and Visitors Center—Philadelphia, Pennsylvania
David W. Graf, Tower Clock Restoration and Repair—Kittery Point, Maine
Reverend Randy Greene and Garrett Law, Abbeville United Methodist Church—Abbeville, Alabama
Richard and Elaine Hamner, Church of the Nativity—Huntsville, Alabama
Janet Hobbs and John Hixson, Saint James Episcopal Church—Cambridge, Massachusetts
Karen Horton, archivist, and Robin Rockstall, facility manager, Roman Catholic Archdiocese of Mobile
Sidney Victor Hulslander, in memoriam—Gainesville, Florida
Gina Johnson and Glenn Long, First United Methodist Church of Tuscaloosa
Reverend Robert McMicken and Mike Mosely, Sampey Memorial Baptist Church—Ramer, Alabama
Dr. Cathy McFadden, Joseph Trimble and Bright Bozeman, Old Ship of Zion AME Church—Montgomery, Alabama
Margaret McGough and Katie McGough Smith—Gainesville, Alabama
Reverend E. Baxter Morris and Rose Frye, First Baptist Church Ripley—Montgomery, Alabama
Karren Pell, author—Montgomery, Alabama
Jimmy Rane, president, and Jennifer Tharpe, Great Southern Wood Preserving—Abbeville, Alabama

Acknowledgements

Marla Reis, Christ Church Cathedral—Mobile, Alabama
Dr. Harald Rohlig, in memoriam, and Mrs. Rohlig—Montgomery, Alabama
Mr. Rod Henderson, in memoriam—Alexander City, Alabama
Patti Shoemaker, church administrator, and Mike Talley, facility manager, First Baptist Church—Montgomery, Alabama
Edwin and Evelyn Stickney, in memoriam—Boston, Massachusetts
Reverend Cooper Stinson, Ramer United Methodist Church—Ramer, Alabama
Reverend Leodis Strong, Brown Chapel AME Church—Selma, Alabama
Michael Tullier, director of marketing and communications, Tuskegee University—Tuskegee, Alabama
Reverend Dr. Luk de Volder and Reverend Kyle Pederson, Trinity Church on the Green—New Haven, Connecticut
Reverend Jonathan Yarboro, First Presbyterian Church—Wetumpka, Alabama
Lawrence Zaborski—West Roxbury, Massachusetts
Nina Zannieri, executive director, and Patrick Leehey, Paul Revere Memorial Association—Boston, Massachusetts

Institutions

Alabama Bicentennial Commission
Alabama Department of Archives and History—Montgomery, Alabama
Alabama Historical Commission—Montgomery, Alabama
Barganier Davis Williams Architects—Montgomery, Alabama
Birmingham Public Library—Birmingham, Alabama
Cathedral Basilica Church of the Immaculate Conception—Mobile, Alabama
City of Saint Jude Catholic Church—Montgomery, Alabama
Dexter King Memorial Baptist Church—Montgomery, Alabama
Episcopal Archdiocese of Mobile
First Presbyterian Church—Greensboro, Alabama
Gainesville Presbyterian Church—Gainesville, Alabama
Holt Street Baptist Church—Montgomery, Alabama
Jamaica Plains Unitarian Universalist Church—Jamaica Plains, Massachusetts
The Mohawk-Hudson Industrial Gateway Museum—Troy, New York
Mount Zion AME Zion Church—Montgomery, Alabama
Sampey Memorial Baptist Church—Ramer, Alabama
Sixteenth Street Baptist Church—Birmingham, Alabama

Introduction
BEGINNINGS AND DISCOVERIES

FIRST IMPRESSIONS AND EARLY EXPERIENCES

*I*n writing a book about historic bells in Alabama, one of the first questions I asked myself was why am I so interested in steeples, towers, tower clocks and bells? After more than a half century of living, I still don't know why. But I do think I know how it began and, more importantly, when it began. I was born in and grew up in the West End neighborhood of Birmingham, Alabama. To this day, I cherish the wonderful memories of my early life in that beautiful neighborhood, which is most commonly associated with being the home of Legion Field, Elmwood Cemetery and Baptist Medical Center-Princeton, which was known then as West End Baptist Hospital when I came into this world.

Our street was Fifteenth Way Southwest. This is the street where my introduction to bells began two years after I was born. I have a memory of taking a walk with my mother and older brother in the neighborhood one day. We walked toward the railroad tracks and Lew Fadely's Drugstore, and as we crested the hill, our church, Beverly United Methodist, came into view. I remember seeing workmen on the roof of the church fellowship hall and stacks of roofing shingles and construction equipment in the yard. At the same moment, my eyes caught sight of a crane hoisting a church bell up and toward the tower. "Look Tom, there's the bell," were the words I remember from my mother—words that have remained with me to this day and which, I believe, defined the beginning of a lifetime of interest and love for bells and towers. With intense fascination, I spotted the workmen up in the tower's belfry openings motioning to the crane operator while a man with a long

Introduction

Beverly United Methodist Church, West End neighborhood, Birmingham, Alabama. *From Birmingham Public Library Archives.*

rope stood on the ground and held the bell steady to keep it from hitting the tower as it was being guided in. It's a sight I will never forget. A couple of years or so later, when the church was completed, we were walking from the church's fellowship hall to the sanctuary when the booming sound of the big bell ringing out from the tower shocked me out of my wits and made me jump! I was not used to the loud sound and impact from the big bell. As I looked toward the tower and its metal louvers, there was a mystery and so many questions about that bell: what was it like inside the tower? How far did the bell swing to make a sound? Was it hung very high in the tower? How do you get up into the tower to see the bell?

So much to wonder about both then and now. Nothing has changed—from that moment on, it seemed that every time my mother took us somewhere in the car, I was always peering out of the bulbous rear window of the old Ford we had at that time. In many instances I was lying down on the seat and looking at all of the church steeples along the way from West End to downtown Birmingham, where I would see even more church towers and steeples. I was always looking for the bell, though some steeples did not have bells, and I always wondered why. It soon became a keen interest to try to see the bells in towers and steeples. If we were approaching a downtown church in Birmingham, the chances were much better of sighting the bell when we were some distance away from an open belfry of a tower rather than up close, as the law of perspective would not permit a view up close.

One of my favorite memories is seeing the bell of the Saint Elias Maronite Church in the steeple with the glowing neon cross when my mother was driving near Eighth Avenue South on a cloudy, rainswept day. After a while I became familiar with most of the downtown churches in Birmingham

Introduction

and could guess which ones had bells behind the louvered openings in the towers or steeples. Some churches had bells on pedestal platforms beside the church and others had bells in bell cotes or in modern armatures. To me, the most interesting ones were always the ones found in the old churches and buildings. I often wondered if the old Terminal Station in Birmingham—designed by the very talented Atlanta architect P. Thornton Mayre—had a bell or bells in either of its twin frontispiece towers. How tragic it is that Mayre's masterpiece did not survive the wrecking ball.

In 1968, we moved to Alexander City, Alabama. Because it was a small town, it didn't take long to find out which churches had bells and which ones didn't. Our church, the First United Methodist Church of Alexander City, had a very large bell in its Romanesque tower. Unfortunately, the rope was broken off at the ceiling and it could not be rung. My continued fascination with the bell, however, gave rise to an idea. My younger brother, David, some friends and I got together a collection to purchase a new rope for the bell, which is still in use today. This opened up a whole new dimension for us as the church bell ringers on Sundays—and at other inappropriate occasions and times, for which we were rightfully admonished! On one such occasion, we were with my mother at the church during the week for a Wesleyan activity and ran off to the tower to ring the bell, loudly and proudly. My mother quickly quelled this action, citing how nearby elderly members had immediately called the church to ask why the bell was ringing at such an hour.

Undaunted, we would still haul on the rope from time to time to feel the tremendous weight and sound of the bell heaving and swaying—sometimes to get a ring and sometimes to just go up in the air from the momentum of the swinging action of the huge bell above us. On Sundays, it was always the church usher who would so kindly tell the young Quasimodos that we had sufficiently announced the call to worship. In 1971, at the end of the summer Vacation Bible School, we had a dream come true: the Reverend Robert Bugg arranged for the church's sexton to bring a ladder into the base of the church tower and let us all go up into the tower to see the bell. I was eleven years old at the time. I remember our friends ascending the ladder to get in the tower. When we got up in the tower, we were all so struck by the bell's massive size and the tremendous air shaft above our heads, where way up top were tower roof joists that supported a midcentury phonograph speaker system that the Reverend Bugg said was silenced after "hillbilly music" was played on it during nocturnal hours. Before seeing the bell for the first time, I always thought it would be placed much higher in the tower and

Introduction

was surprised to see that it was mounted on two large wooden timbers that were supported in the brick masonry walls of the tower slightly below the base of the large wooden louvers. Access to the church tower is not possible at the time of this writing, but I would guess that the bell was likely a forty-inch-diameter C.S. Bell of Hillsborough, Ohio, or quite possibly a Blymer Bell from Cincinnati, or perhaps even a National Bell from Cincinnati.

One of my favorite things to do has always been exploring—even when I was only four or five years old. Stories are told of me "running away from home" at an early age. The accounts are true, and though I knew what I was doing and where I was going and why, my parents taught me very well about never doing those types of prekindergarten excursions again. Still, much of the reason for my young adventures had to do with seeing if I might be able to go to our church and somehow get up in the tower to see the bell—if the church sexton, Isaiah, would let me. The nearby Church of the Blessed Sacrament also held a deep fascination for me. I wondered about whether there was a bell, or bells, in its tall Basilican tower, and during my West End travels, I would always walk by the church, looking up to see what might be in the tower.

I was also fascinated by fire engines and would walk to the West End Fire Station to see the beautiful American LaFrance fire trucks and the firehouse dog, Freckles, who is now buried beside the station. The old fire engines had shiny silver bells, which were always rung along with the station alarm bell when the crews were going to fight a fire. There were other bells, too, such as the bells on trains that rumbled through the crossing at the end of Fifteenth Way Southwest and Pearson Avenue.

As I got older, I continued exploring, often taking either a walk or a bike ride into the neighborhoods and side streets of Alexander City, including bridges and a tunnel under the railroad near the old Hamp Lyon stadium and Junior High School. Of course, finding bells was always in my mind as I rode by churches, stopping to see if they were open and if there was a way to go up in the tower. While walking one day, I noticed a beautiful old African American church that seemed to be falling into disrepair and, naturally, wandered closer to have a look. As I pressed the door of the tower, amazingly, it was open. I cautiously went inside and looked up through the gaps and cracks of the ceiling above and saw the dark, round silhouette directly above—the bell was still in the tower! I think this was the first time I ever thought that a bell might fall on me, so I carefully exited and left the situation as it was before. Years later, the church was demolished, but the bell was saved and is now mounted in front of the new church.

Introduction

Naturally, my interest in bells became a preoccupation through my years of education and learning, segueing right into my parallel interest in architecture, which also began in my early childhood and, I believe, was intrinsically woven into my interest in bells and, a little later on, my fascination with tower clocks. My interest in tower clocks, however, began on a much smaller scale—with a cuckoo clock! On our street in West End, we had a neighbor, Mrs. Roy, who lived just a few houses up from us and had a house with different clocks of all makes and models. These clocks ticktocked and struck the hour in a most fascinating way. When I first visited Mrs. Roy, you can imagine what kind of deep impression this experience had on me. Seeing a grandfather clock's huge pendulum movement and the sound of bells inside striking the hour for the first time was music to my ears. The mystery of how this was accomplished inside a great, tall box was a curiosity for a young boy of three years.

Part of the delightful cacophony were the other clocks she had—most notably her cuckoo clocks, which were a such an amazement to me. I wondered how the little bird knew when to come out of the shuttered window above the clock's numerals and "cuckoo" the hour. Mrs. Roy is to be venerated and honored, especially with the mark of being most patient, as I would ask her to let me see the cuckoo bird again and again by moving the clock hands to the hour mark—especially the twelfth hour. My visits to Mrs. Roy's house to see the clocks were making connections in my mind to the great bell of Beverly United Methodist Church when it struck the hour to call parishioners to worship. Frederick Shelley, in his book, *Early American Tower Clocks*, tells us that the term *clock* originates from the Latin *clocca*, which means bell.

Another key contributor to my early childhood fascination with clocks, and most likely the very origin of my interest in tower clocks, was the Maronite Church of Saint Elias, which was a regular sight during my years growing up in Birmingham. Saint Elias was one of the rare church towers in the city that featured a striking tower clock. Save for the long-since-demolished old city hall, I honestly can't think of any other tower clocks in the area, and tower clock installation records attest to this. The steeple of Saint Elias was something I always looked for whenever we were driving on Eighth Avenue East or Green Springs Highway and, even better, when we traversed right in front of the church on Eighth Street South. I always tried to sit or stand up in the back seat to see that bell in the tower and, as a double-dividend, the tower clock dials. Never underestimate the power of little minds. I can remember wondering, how does the bell ring? How do

Introduction

you get up into the steeple? Where is the ladder that goes up to the clock? How big is the bell? Is it loud? How did they put the bell in the tower? The musings of my mind on the Saint Elias tower, and practically all clock towers, has never changed—only my understanding of them, thanks to my studies in architecture and a lifetime spent working in the profession, including historic preservation and academia.

In addition to providing an in-depth look at Alabama's historic bells during the early years, the Civil War and the civil rights movement, this book shares heartfelt concerns for these very important and significant bells and tower clocks. Namely, they should be rediscovered and appreciated; the towers, steeples, cupolas and domes bearing these instruments should be preserved and restored for complete structural integrity as the armature for these artifacts to perform in; and lastly, technology should become synergistic in preserving and reusing them in their original sites. Horology—the science of clockmaking—and bellmaking, or bell founding, if you will, are two artisan trades that have largely disappeared from United States industry in the twenty-first century, with the exception of a few enduring companies with traditions and legacies in both crafts. Gone are the days, however, of the several mighty foundry furnaces churning out bells for towers and steeples in the United States and beyond. Generally speaking, the same may be said for the striking tower clock industry.

It is still possible to find tower clock makers and bellfounders, but they are not in abundance. They are highly specialized, knowledgeable and very passionate about their crafts, though their products may not be in such great volume as they were during the mid-nineteenth to mid-twentieth centuries—the latter being the time during which most bell foundries went out of business. Why? They simply could not compete with the twentieth-century invention of the electronic chime or carillon, which many churches and institutions began installing in the towers of their new buildings—in the same towers housing the real bells. This was a real tragedy in the United States and in other countries around the globe. The electronic bell system was easier to install and more diverse in the number of musical tune selections that could be broadcast from the tower speakers in all directions. The electronic system meant the death knell for the real, touchable foundry-cast bell, for practical reasons, and the bell-making business has never been the same since.

Tower clocks, however, have endured much longer and have only in recent times begun to suffer the fate of removal from steeples and towers in favor of digital systems, which are purported to keep time to the accuracy

Introduction

of Greenwich Mean Time or the U.S. Naval Observatory's standards. It is neither wise nor prudent to deny or denigrate progress in technology. Indeed, it has improved our standard of living and quality of life in so many areas that are unfathomable to measure. Anyone with an understanding of archival construction conditions who observes the interior of a tower that is 80 to 150 years old—or older—will understand concerns about the condition of the finite materials that support the timepieces, stationary clock bells and swing-ringing bells, no matter how large or small the bells may be. Even if the bells are mute and no longer ring, the static weight of the bell is a concern, and the vintage striking tower clocks are no exception. A steeple with a small- or moderate-sized bell and the hardware needed to make it ring can easily weigh nearly a ton. Clock towers with a striking tower clock and a stationary striking bell mounted in the tower can support more weight, even much more, depending on the size of the bell.

In yesteryear, when weights were used to wind up the timepiece, the tonnage of the clock weights alone was enormous, and it was dangerous if the weights ever broke free from the ropes or cables. The same goes for the typical striking tower clock pendulum that weighs more than a hundred pounds, which is why the clockmakers had catch floors and chutes built just below the clock. Heavy timber beam construction, which has carried the load of many trains with boxcars over railroad bridges and trestles, has been the mainstay support of all early United States architecture, such as log cabins, timber houses and clock and bell towers. But consider what time, heat, moisture and pigeon guano can do to heavy timber construction over a century or more. In some instances, the materials perform well under the ideal circumstances, so there is something to be said for the innate properties of archival building materials. But the situation becomes a very grave concern when water, fowl or rodents enter the structure. Even still, concerning bells, there is another factor at work within the very assembly of the bell and its enabling hardware—the corrosion of the principal bolt that fastens the bell to its yoke, due to the use of two dissimilar metals, bronze and cast iron. This effect, over time, can cause the bolt to deteriorate into a stalactite in the middle of the principal bolt's shaft, which is extremely dangerous because the bell could fall at any moment. Not to be an alarmist regarding this concern, but rather to be aware of this as a possibility, being cautious and safe is the best approach. It's even more reason to have towers and bells inspected and maintained—the term preservationists use is "regular cyclical maintenance" guided by reasonableness and common sense.

Introduction

At the time of this writing, reports of bells falling from or through towers is rare, though it has happened on occasion. Still, there is yet another concern. In a number of observed cases, a single tower bell's mounts on either side of the bell—known as A-Mounts (or A-Stands, either is correct)—which support the bell and its yoke, and the great rope-wheel have been noted to have been braced by two-by-four-inch wood studs fixed against the walls or beams to prevent them from falling over and tumbling headlong down the tower shaft toward disaster. Conditions like these are more numerous than expected. How and why do such conditions develop and remain unresolved, even in our great state of Alabama? There are no easy answers, but we may hypothesize and come close to the nature of these problems, which is that authentic clocks and bells are no longer prominent, and they are heard much less in our day than before. Because they are not heard, they are not seen, and when they are not seen, they become the case of the adage "out of sight, out of mind."

However, and thankfully, the sound of an hour strike or Westminster peal is still heard in cities and counties where the historic city hall or county courthouse—and the original striking tower clock—has been preserved. In times past, striking tower clocks generally kept time with a margin of error, and it was not unusual to observe differences in the time told from clockface to clockface in any town or city where there were multiple tower clocks. High winds could also affect the hands of a clock, but the heavy torque of the clock's gears could generally resist most wind conditions unless they were very severe. It must be said that these tower clocks were wonderfully made and tuned to precision. If any reader has ever had a chance to observe an original striking tower clock with a pendulum movement, you know they are a wonder to behold. One of the great joys of doing the research for this book has been finding the many treasures hiding in Alabama steeples and towers during my tower climbs, as well as from oral history and archival information.

I will let the towers speak for themselves in revealing the treasures they possess, but for now, let me say that Alabama has been very blessed with the very best, unique and rare bells from historic bell foundries in the United States and beyond, as well as a treasure-trove of antique and rare tower clocks from the most significant and historic American clockmakers. It is my hope that you may gain such an appreciation of Alabama's striking tower clock and bell heritage that all such artifacts within our state—especially those that are silent or broken—may once again tell time, strike the hour, announce worship services and weddings, mournfully honoring the departed, holidays, special occasions, the end of wars and all other events and celebrations.

May this continue to be so, both now and into tomorrow.

1

EARLY BELLS OF ALABAMA

Territory, Statehood, Frontier and Antebellum

*T*here is hardly any mention of bells found anywhere in historical narratives from the time of the advent of Alabama as a territory in 1817, and for good reason—they were not as abundant in America as they became later on. During this era in our nation, Colonel Aaron Hobart, Benjamin and Julius Hanks, George R. and George H. Holbrook and Paul Revere were among the few bellfounders in the United States, and they were the ones that really mattered. When Alabama was becoming an official territory, there was no capitol building for representatives to meet in. They only had the space afforded to the temporary government in the Douglass Hotel on High Street in old Saint Stephens, the first capital city of the Alabama territory.

In 1819, when delegates gathered for the Territorial Constitution Convention in Huntsville to draft a state constitution to meet the congressional requirements for gaining statehood and admission to the Union, they met in a wood frame assembly hall, which was later demolished but wonderfully rebuilt in our time as the centerpiece of Constitution Village in Huntsville.

When the state capital was moved to Cahawba, a new statehouse was built to order, and it did include a steeple, which was referred to as a dome in previous accounts, very likely because of its bell-shaped roof. The statehouse was constructed in 1820 by the Crocheron family of Staten Island, New York. It was built as a Federal-style building, according to construction specifications, artist depictions and eyewitness accounts. It is hard to know

Above: Lafayette's Bell, circa 1820. *From Alabama Department of Archives and History.*

Left: Constitution Hall Park, Huntsville, Alabama. *From Alabama Department of Archives and History.*

for certain if there was a bell hanging in the statehouse dome or steeple, though it is entirely possible that evidence confirming or denying the presence of a bell in the first state capitol building might yet be revealed in some wonderful or mysterious way—perhaps through the emergence of a previously unknown document or state record. In the event that there was a bell, it would have likely been one of a very rare mark, perhaps a Hanks, Holbrook, Revere or early Andrew Meneely bell—all of these being among the earliest bells cast in our nation since the Revolution and the establishment of the United States as a sovereign nation.

Though we would all like to believe that the bells from the Hanks, Holbrook, Revere and Meneely bell foundries were cast for Alabama churches and institutions, it stands to reason that many of the bells that were cast for use in Alabama during this era were likely steamboat bells, fire bells, plantation bells, railroad bells and perhaps small church bells. Most bells were probably small to medium size and used for transportation and alarms and to announce the worship hour.

Nonetheless, with regard to Alabama's first capital and statehouse—bell or no bell—because of problems with the rivers rising and flooding in

Old statehouse in Cahawba, circa 1820. *From Alabama Department of Archives and History.*

Christian Methodist Episcopal Church with the old statehouse dome mounted on top. *From the author.*

Cahawba, the state capital was once again moved, this time to Tuscaloosa. This resulted in a period of decline for Cahawba, and many of the buildings were affected by the flooding, including the capitol. Many were eventually dismantled for their bricks and other elements for reuse elsewhere, but not before being visited by the Revolutionary War hero Marquis de Lafayette in 1825. He was given a hero's welcome and grand reception at Cahawba following his visit to Montgomery, where he was also feted with much grandiosity and pomp and honored by the ringing of the handle-mounted old ship's bell, which was called Alabama's Liberty Bell at the time but is now known as the Lafayette Bell.

Around 1830, Major William Robinson, owner of a large plantation in Lowndesboro, assembled a team of six pairs of oxen and hauled the Cahawba capitol dome from the former state capitol building to the Methodist church in Lowndesboro, where it was installed atop the church and remains to this very day. In 1866, the church was deeded to the Christian Methodist Episcopal (CME) Church, an African American denomination. They assembled for services in the building for the better part of the next 120 years and enjoyed the use of a rare and unique Regester and Webb bronze church bell, which was cast in Baltimore, Maryland, in 1858. The bell was not the same one that hung in the dome when it was on the statehouse at Cahawba and was likely procured by the congregation a decade before the church was deeded to the CME congregation.

Regester and Webb bells are very rare, and the company was said to have been chiefly known for supplying ships with bells. Around this time, a young, enterprising Irishman named Henry McShane began working for Joshua Regester—McShane being someone we will learn more about later in our story. The Regester and Webb bell at the CME Church in Lowndesboro is the only one identified in Alabama as of this writing and seems to be a departure for the Regester and Webb bellmakers because of its larger size and the presence of its mounting and swing-ringing hardware—atypical for ship's bells, which are mounted in a stationary fashion and rung by hand from a clapper rope.

The new capitol building in Tuscaloosa was designed by architect William Nichols and was a wonderful Georgian imitation of an Ithiel Town or James Dakin public building design. Photographs of this building depict a primitive bell cote situated next to the dome. Questions arise as to whether the bell cote was original to the design, or if it was an afterthought. Nonetheless, this capitol did have a bell, and from photographs, it appears to have been an iron bell of average size. Depending on when it was placed on the capitol, it could have been from any of the aforementioned bellfounders, or James P.

Inscription on the rare 1858 Regester and Webb bell that is hanging in the dome of the Christian Methodist Episcopal Church. *From Ryan Schlesinger.*

HISTORIC ALABAMA BELLS

The 1858 Regester and Webb bell hanging in the dome of the Christian Methodist Episcopal Church, Lowndesboro, Alabama. *From Ryan Schlesinger.*

Allaire's Howell Works. The original bell of Saint John's Episcopal Church in Montgomery was cast by Allaire in the 1840s and was quite large and perhaps made of iron.

Overarching the categories of Alabama as a territory and state, there is the category of Alabama as a frontier. This category applies to the geographical domain of Alabama prior to, during and after achieving the chronological designations as a territory and state. We may think of Mobile and its rich and storied history under the flags of Spain, France and Britain and ponder whether any Spanish, French or English bells were in the city or area before the territorial or statehood milestones. It is the belief of this author that there were bells; however, due to a lack of identification or authentication of such bells, the assumption would be that the bells have been lost or possibly yet undiscovered. It would seem that there would have to be sunken ships in Mobile Bay and the Gulf with bells on board. There are likely many readers who know of the whereabouts of such artifacts, whether they lie sunken on the ocean floor of the Gulf or the bay, or perhaps, in various points along Alabama's steamboat waterways of long ago. We may also think of

The 1829 state capitol in Tuscaloosa with its bell atop the portico. *From Historic American Buildings Survey—Historic American Engineering Record, Library of Congress.*

the patterns of settlement in Alabama where the early pioneers first staked out lands, towns and cities to build their primitive dwellings, structures, town buildings and houses of worship out of wood. Did any bells appear in Alabama during this time? Probably, but more on the order of smaller bells made of iron or brass, which were family heirlooms or belongings prior to coming to Alabama. It is very probable that many an iron farm bell served as a church bell in its new life in Alabama.

The story of Williamson Hawkins and how this hardy pioneer's new life began in Jones Valley emerges to the forefront of our discussion about the frontier era of Alabama. Born in Beaufort, South Carolina, in 1790, Williamson Hawkins served in the War of 1812, fighting the Creek Indians in the Mississippi Territory—most notably at the Battle of Horseshoe Bend near Dadeville, Alabama. It is believed that the troops marched from their station in Tennessee through the northern territory, passing through the Jones Valley on their way to battle.

The general thought among those studying Hawkins was that this lush, forested valley made such a huge impression on him that he decided to settle

Williamson Hawkins, early settler of Jones Valley and donor of Saint John's Episcopal Church bell. *From Birmingham Public Library.*

down for life. It was, in the words of those who witnessed it first, a land "full of fish and fowl" with running streams of crystal-clear water. It has been said that Williamson Hawkins, who was described as a "stoutly built man," upon putting down roots in this land with his wife, Betsy, after the war, settled the area with "gun and axe" beginning around the year 1815. He eventually grew his lands into a plantation and garnered tremendous wealth, principally as a cotton grower—with slave labor, of course—but his lasting legacy is that of a kind and benevolent slaveholder.

In 1850, Connecticut native Maria Welton, soon to become Williamson's daughter-in-law, founded Saint John's Episcopal Church in Elyton with other local Jones Valley families. Williamson and Betsy became members of this church, and the parishioners met at Jefferson Academy and at one another's homes for several years after the church was founded. Life in Jones Valley was blissful during this time, but toward the end of the Civil War, Union troops occupied the Hawkins plantation, to his daily consternation; he experienced severe losses after the troops left. This unfortunate event might offer some explanation for why their beloved Saint John's church had no church building or bell.

Perhaps it was when Williamson Hawkins had recovered from the war in 1871 that he donated a parcel of land for the church and made arrangements for a Carpenter Gothic sanctuary in Ashville to be moved to Elyton by oxen. In 1872, at age eighty-two, he gifted the church a 484-pound brass bell from the prized Jones and Company Bell Foundry in Troy, New York. This was one of the best bellmakers in the nation at that time and is still considered to be among the ranks of the most excellent bells and in the category of rare and historic bells among those in the bell industry as well as historians and collectors. On the Hawkins bell, the inscription "Troy Bell Foundry" is above "Jones and Company," which is an interesting motif that identified the foundry's company era as opposed to when it was known as "Jones and Hitchcock" and referred to principally as the "Troy Bell Foundry." Though this bell comes at a much later time in Alabama's history, the fact that it came from one of Alabama's earliest frontier settlers, though delayed due to the onset and trials of the Civil

Saint John's Episcopal Church, Elyton, Alabama. *From O. V. Hunt Collection, Birmingham Public Library Archives.*

War, makes it more fitting that the story is told here. No doubt, a bell was on Williamson Hawkins's mind to complete the realization of St. John's Church, which would have very likely transpired well before the Civil War.

The most prevalent question that comes to mind regarding this time period is what and where is the oldest surviving bell in Alabama? To be very honest, I don't know the answer to that question, but it is my hope that this book will create and foster an interest in bells that will lead to answers to questions like this. Further, it is my hope that this work will prove me wrong about conjectures I have made regarding the number of rare and unusual bells in our great state. I am not afraid of this—in fact, I welcome any research that proves there are more historic bells in Alabama. That would only increase our state's stature as a land where early citizens knew quality and excellence and sought after such in generous measures and gestures for fellow neighbors, churches and communities.

Returning to the question regarding the oldest bell in Alabama, maybe we should refine the question: what and where is the oldest tower bell in Alabama? I think this is the question we are really asking because tower bells are usually of a nominal size and graduate upward in terms of size and

Left: The Williamson Hawkins bell for Saint John's Episcopal Church cast by the Troy Bell Foundry, Troy, New York. *From Lindsay Elliot, Vulcan Park, Birmingham.*

Below: Detail of the inscription of Saint John's Episcopal Church bell. *From Lindsay Elliot, Vulcan Park, Birmingham.*

Cathedral Basilica of the Immaculate Conception, Mobile, Alabama. *From the archives of the Archdiocese of Mobile, Karen Horton, archivist.*

weight, and the date of casting is embedded into the bell itself, along with the name and city of the bellfounder.

The fact remains—unique and rare bells have made their way to Alabama from some of the most respected bellfounders in our nation's history. In the following chapters, we shall discover more about these masters of the art, science and craft of casting bells and how they also tell the story of Alabama.

In our search for the oldest bell—or bells—Mobile is a good place to start. According to Karen Horton, archivist for the Archdiocese of Mobile,

> *The cathedral is the oldest. It was a parish beginning in 1703, then a part of the Diocese of Quebec. Over the years, the parish continued to exist under different dioceses, including the Archdiocese of Baltimore and for a*

few years the Diocese of Havana and then the Archdiocese of New Orleans. When we were named a diocese in 1829, the Mobile parish became the cathedral parish for the Diocese of Mobile. So, my point is the parish preceded the designation of cathedral parish and was the parish of Our Lady of the Holy Conception before that (name changed slightly, depending on which country was in control of Mobile at the time).

Surely there were bells here, but have they survived and are they in someone's possession now? We may never know. Nonetheless, the cathedral was built in two stages: the basilica proper was built first, and the towers and the portico were constructed in the 1880s. There is a bell in the north tower that is referred to as the "1876 Bell," which was cast by the McShane Bell Foundry in 1876. To reach the bell, one must climb the original forty-foot ladder, which goes straight up the tower wall to the belfry.

The second-oldest church in the Archdiocese of Mobile was the Church of Saint Vincent de Paul, now known as Prince of Peace Catholic Church. Its first structure was built in 1847 and was replaced by the second, and present, sanctuary, which was designed by James H. Hutchisson and completed in 1877. The bell of the former Saint Vincent de Paul was cast by the McShane Bell Foundry of Baltimore, Maryland, in 1881 and is one of the state's largest swing-ringing bells. It likely weighs four thousand pounds, or approximately two tons. The first structure may have had a bell, but at present, it is difficult to confirm this.

The 1876 bell in the Cathedral Basilica of the Immaculate Conception, Mobile, Alabama. *From the archives of the Archdiocese of Mobile, Karen Horton, archivist.*

The Episcopal Church figures greatly in the historical narrative of Alabama before, during and after statehood, especially given our quest for finding the earliest and oldest bells. The oldest episcopal church in Alabama is Christ Church Cathedral in Mobile, which was designed and constructed in 1840 in the style of Greek Revival and was topped with a 167-foot steeple, which crashed into the sanctuary during a hurricane in 1906. Unbelievably, the church bell, a Meneely West Troy bell from 1847,

Saint Vincent de Paul Church, now known as Prince of Peace Catholic Church, Mobile, Alabama. *From the archives of the Archdiocese of Mobile, Karen Horton, archivist.*

which weighed more than a ton, survived the fall and is now located at the front right pillar of the church's entrance. After more than one hundred years, the congregation of Christ Church Cathedral desired to once again place the steeple back on the church and went to work to make the dream a reality. On Sunday, April 23, 2017, Christ Church celebrated its first worship service with the new historically accurate

Reverend John Basiimwa looking over the 1887 McShane bell. *From the archives of the Archdiocese of Mobile, Karen Horton, archivist.*

Left: Christ Cathedral Episcopal Church's reconstructed steeple in 2017. *From Marla Reis, Christ Cathedral.*

Below: Illustration of Saint Luke's Episcopal Church by Anna M. Vassar in 1872. *From Old Cahawba Archeological Park, Alabama Department of Archives and History.*

Left: The large 1847 Meneely West Troy bell that survived the toppling of the steeple in the hurricane of 1906. *From Marla Reis, Christ Cathedral.*

Below: The cast steel alloy bell found in the attic of Saint Luke's Episcopal Church while readying for the move back to Old Cahawba. *From Linda Derry, Old Cahawba Archaeological Park.*

Saint Luke's Episcopal Church, Old Cahawba, 2019. *From Jonathan Matthews, Old Cahawba Archaeological Park.*

reconstructed steeple—an exact aesthetic replica of the original steeple that was destroyed.

Leading this architectural initiative for Christ Cathedral Church was Montgomery architect James I. Barganier, who studied archival drawings and documents to get the scale, details and look to be true to the style and period. In the process, he learned that the steeple's original cross was sixteen feet tall, and he used this to create the appropriate scale and proportion of the tower, remarking quite profoundly and ecclesiastically that "the Cross led the way."

The second-oldest episcopal church in Alabama is Saint Luke's Episcopal Church of Old Cahawba (also spelled *Cahaba*), which was built in 1854 from New York architect Richard Upjohn's *Rural Architecture* book of plans, though it was modified to suit the congregation of Cahawba. In 1876, the church was moved to Martin's Station, where it remained until the mid-2000s, when it was moved back to Cahawba by the Rural Studio of Auburn University's College of Architecture Design and Construction. During the move, a bell was discovered in the attic of church. Cast by C.S. Bell of Hillsborough, Ohio, it was not the original bell in the Upjohn tower, but it is significant to the church's history.

Madison County courthouse in the 1840s. *From Historic American Buildings Survey—Historic American Engineering Record, Library of Congress.*

The 1849 clock bell cast by T.I. Dyre Jr. of Brass and Bell Foundry of Philadelphia, Pennsylvania. *From the author.*

One of the rarest bells, and among the earliest bells, is the 1840 Madison County Courthouse clock bell, which was recently rediscovered in Huntsville. The bell was part of the striking tower clock made by J.D. Custer of Norristown, Pennsylvania, which was installed in the Choragic Monument of Lysicrates lantern atop the courthouse in 1849. This rare bell was cast in 1849 by T.I. Dyre Jr. of Philadelphia, Pennsylvania, and is believed to be the only one in Alabama that was cast by the T.I. Dyre Brass and Bell Foundry.

2
PAUL REVERE

REVOLUTIONARY WAR HERO, COPPERSMITH AND BELLMAKER

Paul Revere's father was the great-grandson of a Huguenot refugee who fled from France to Holland and then to the Isle of Guernsey. In 1715, at the age of thirteen, he was sent from Guernsey to Boston by his Uncle Simon. He was to become a goldsmith's apprentice. The real name of this young man was Apollos Rivoire, but because so many people in Boston had difficulty pronouncing his given French name, he changed it to Paul Revere. He became Paul Revere I, and his marital union produced twelve children, including the renowned Paul Revere. As the third child of the twelve, he was named after his father and became Paul Revere II.

Born on January 1, 1735, in Boston's North End, Paul Revere was baptized in the New Brick Meeting-House and attended the North Grammar School on North Bennett Street. Upon finishing school, he began to work as a metalsmith apprentice for his father. An able and artistic apprentice, Paul Revere became adept with the pencil and the graving tool, making all kinds of excellent metal wares, such as kettles, cups, spoons, pitchers and mugs. These priceless items are still in New England households today and are highly prized. In this stage of young Revere's life, we find the beginnings of his later work casting bells and making large copper products. As with everything he set his hand to, the mark of excellence was on all that he undertook. As a young man of twenty-two, he was commissioned as a second lieutenant in the artillery of the Massachusetts Bay Colony and fought against the French at Crown Point.

Paul Revere. *From Music Division, New York Public Library Digital Collections.*

After the conflict ended, he married Sarah Orne, and in 1762, they began their domestic life together in a house on Fish Street near Clark's Wharf. They joined the New Brick Meeting-House, which was at the corner of Richmond and Middle Streets, and the two were active members of the congregation. Revere engraved the colony's seal and the copper plates for printing the colony's money. His outstanding copper tea kettles and silver tea pots made him well known, and as he became increasingly prosperous, he bought a house on North Square in the aristocratic section of Boston. Revere lived in this house during the Revolution.

Paul Revere was a colonial patriot, if there ever was one, before the Revolution. He drew political cartoons that ridiculed George III and his agents in America, joined the Sons of Liberty and was an active participant in the Boston Tea Party. From 1774 to 1775, Paul Revere was employed as an express rider for the Boston Committee of Correspondence and the Massachusetts Committee of Safety. He carried the copies of articles and documents as well as urgent news and messages. It was on one such ride to Philadelphia that he was afforded an opportunity to study a powder mill and learned how to cast cannons.

Most Americans connect Paul Revere with his famous and celebrated Midnight Ride to Lexington on the night of April 18, 1775. Very likely, fewer Americans know much about his ride to Lexington two days earlier, which certain scholars have regarded as the more important of the two. More than thirty towns were stirred into a state of readiness for the British troops coming on their way to Lexington and Concord to fight on the nineteenth.

Revere's military service during the war included repairing disabled cannons and working as an armor-plate contractor. He also supplied several thousand pounds of sheet copper for gunships and copper and brass for the frigate ship *Constitution*.

Around 1800, Paul Revere bought an old government powder mill to establish a copper rolling mill and foundry for coppering roofs—like the Massachusetts Statehouse—and casting bells and cannons. How Revere came to cast his very first bell is an interesting story, as the bell itself has had quite a history and longevity of use. This bell saw service in the Old North Meeting House—replacing that church's original bell—before it was obtained by the New Brick Meeting-House congregation, where it rang to awaken citizens in the morning and send them to bed in the evening. It also rang to close the market; to announce the Lord's Day for services; and for weddings, funerals and festivals. This fine, old, five-hundred-pound bell was a faithful servant at the New Brick Meeting-House for many years, but one day in 1792, the old bell cracked, inciting discussion among church leaders that the bell should be sent to England to be melted down and recast.

Paul Revere, a respected member of this church, heard this news and immediately inquired about trying his hand at recasting the bell, though he had practically no prior experience in casting bells. It is believed that Revere wanted to cast bells for some time and saw a great opportunity in the moment. Revere first consulted with one of, if not possibly the first bell caster in the United States, Colonel Aaron Hobart, before undertaking the

The first bell made by Paul Revere. Cast in 1792, it is now in residence at Saint James Episcopal Church in Cambridge, Massachusetts. *From Janet Hobbs and John Hixson.*

work of actually recasting the bell. Hobart's mentorship and help became extremely beneficial to Revere in remaking this bell, which was believed to have been cast in England around 1650. The recasting effort was successful, and although the bell was recast at 912 pounds—almost twice its original size—it was remade very decently, though the musical tonality of the bell was somewhat lacking, as was the case with all of Revere's early bells. This prompted one member of the clergy to remark, "That although we may be thankful for Mr. Revere being able to cast Bells, we may not always be thankful for the sound that they make." This clergyman's commentary, obviously spoken too soon, was not to be the last word on the quality of the sound of the Revere bells.

In 1871, the New Brick Meeting-House was taken down, and the bell was stored in a loft for the better part of thirty years. It was then sold to the congregation of Saint James Episcopal Church in Cambridge, Massachusetts, where it remains today in a place of honor in the sanctuary beside the church's parishioners near the lectern. Since acquiring the bell around the turn of the twentieth century, Saint James has been a faithful steward of the most critical and important artifact from the life and work of Paul Revere—beautifully preserved for posterity and appreciation by future generations.

3
CAST BY PAUL REVERE AND SON

THE FIRST UNITED METHODIST CHURCH OF TUSCALOOSA BELL

*D*uring the late eighteenth and early nineteenth centuries, the American Methodist Church was being expanded to the "Old Southwest" by the itinerant ministry of the Methodist Circuit Riders—referred to as the "pioneer preachers" by Theodore Roosevelt. The Tuscaloosa Methodist Church, as it was originally chartered, was organized in 1818, and the Reverend Ebenezer Hearn was installed as the first minister of the church. According to church history, the first structure was built on the present site in 1834 and included the highly prized, historic, significant and rare church bell, which was cast by Revere Boston in 1828. This was the foundry established by the Revolutionary War hero, coppersmith and bell foundryman Paul Revere. Upon his death in 1818, he was succeeded by his sons and grandsons as well as key company personnel, including company agent Henry N. Hooper and the master bell-casting artisan, William Blake.

The First United Methodist Church of Tuscaloosa bell is one of the last bells cast by Paul Revere and Son before Hooper acquired the foundry and its associated copperworks in 1828 (some accounts list the date of acquisition as 1829) through a difficult legal battle with the Revere family. The most authoritative scholarly research done by Edward and Evelyn Stickney, authors of *The Bells of Paul Revere, His Sons, and His Grandsons*, the definitive book on Revere bells, state that the foundry belonged to the Reveres in 1828. Nonetheless, there is no doubt that the First United Methodist Church of Tuscaloosa bell was either cast, or closely overseen, by William Blake—the man responsible for establishing the rich and full

The First United Methodist Church of Tuscaloosa with its steeple—where the Revere bell resides—in the background. *From the author.*

musical quality and tonality of the Revere bells. Eventually, William Blake would play a greater role in the history of the bell foundry. To date, foundry records primarily propose that the Tuscaloosa United Methodist Church bell is believed to be the only bell in the state cast by Revere Boston when it was owned by the Revere family—possessing the Revere name on its crown, it is the genuine Revere article.

We may all thank Bishop Clare Purcell, who was serving as the pastor of the First Methodist Church of Tuscaloosa when the old church sanctuary was torn down in 1920, for noticing the bell. The bell was sadly left in a trash pile when the Reverend Purcell immediately had it removed, refurbished, cleaned and mounted in a rear hall of the Sunday School building before it was hung in the church tower.

Katie Bell Harrison confirmed the significance of the bell after the Reverend Purcell had saved it from certain harm and loss. In time, Harrison even made contact with E.H.R. Revere of Boston, a descendent of Paul Revere, to discover more information about the bell and whether it was indeed the only one in Alabama.

Left: The 1828 Revere and Son bell from the First United Methodist Church of Tuscaloosa. *From the author.*

Below: The Revere Boston inscription on the Revere bell. *From the author.*

The inscription on the bell below the crown reads:

Revere Boston

*Presented by Samuel Saint John Jr. and Joshua Leavens of Mobile
To The Methodist Episcopal Church Tuscaloosa Alabama*

What is amazing about this Revere bell is that there is no date of its casting on the inscription, meaning that the burden of proof is in the record of its casting and shipping to Mobile before the rest of the journey upriver to Tuscaloosa. Most Revere bells do have a casting date inscribed on them, yet there is also nuance in how the Revere bells are titled, even when they are believed to have been cast by George Holbrook—a conversation for another day and time.

As to the question of whether this Revere bell is, in fact, the only one of its kind in Alabama, one historical entry suggests that there was another Revere bell meant for Alabama, but it sank in the river with the vessel transporting it. The location is unknown. E.H.R. Revere replied to Harrison by letter confirming that the shipping records of Paul Revere and Son did list a bell shipped to Mobile in September 1828, and there were no other bells listed as being shipped to Alabama, which seems to confirm that the Revere bell in Tuscaloosa is very likely the only one in the state.

In this narrative about the special bell from Boston, there are so many individuals who have contributed to the history and preservation of the Revere bell. Time and space would not permit to list them here, but they are commemorated in the archives of the Tuscaloosa United Methodist Church. Among those included are Miss Jane Smallwood, who rang the bell for the church; Ms. Smallwoods's Sunday school class, which contributed so much toward the preservation of the bell; Loula Hargrove of Montgomery; and so many others.

The bell also attracted the attention of the nation's most incomparable Revere bell historians and scholars: the late Edwin and Evelyn Stickney, authors of the 1976 classic *The Bells of Paul Revere, His Sons, and His Grandsons*. The Stickneys were fascinated by the Revere bell that made it to Alabama, and after visiting the church to see and study the bell, they kept regular correspondence in the years that followed and were a great help to the author in ways innumerable with respect to the Tuscaloosa bell and beyond.

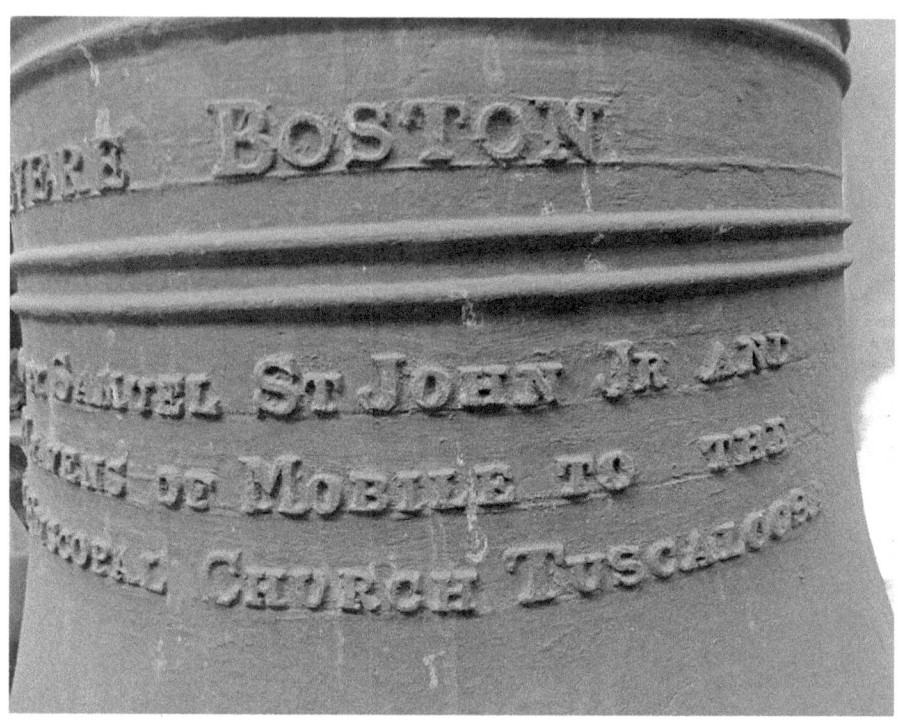

Above: The inscription bearing the names of donors of the Revere bell. *From the author.*

Left: A view of the rear of the Revere bell. Curiously, no casting date appears anywhere on the bell. *From the author.*

The First United Methodist Church of Tuscaloosa is so very fortunate to have this special treasure of American history within the tall steeple of its beautiful church. The connections this bell makes with so much that is "America" are due in large part to Paul Revere, great patriot that he was—a son of the Revolution, man of faith, excellent coppersmith and bellmaker extraordinaire.

4
HENRY N. HOOPER AND COMPANY, BOSTON

Successor to Paul Revere and Son, Boston

There is only one important name besides that of William Blake, the master bellfounder of Revere and Son, and that is Henry Northey Hooper, company agent for Revere and Son and Copperworks Boston. He was the successor of Revere and Son in 1830, though it is believed that the acquisition occurred around 1828 or 1829. Many biographical sketches show him as an apprentice of Paul Revere—the original founder. Not likely.

Since Hooper was born on July 16, 1799, in Manchester-by-the-Sea, Massachusetts, and given that Paul Revere cast his last bell around 1811, it seems unlikely that Hooper would have apprenticed under the senior Revere, though it is not impossible. What appears to be more likely, and highly plausible, is that Hooper entered the Revere business in adulthood, and whatever his station was within the company at the first, he emerged as a tremendous businessman with incredible instincts and intuition for marketing, promoting and selling the wares of Revere and Son. In so many words, he was a "rainmaker" with a gift for great communication and public relations.

Hooper appears to have been indispensable to the company, and without him, the business surely would not have had the success it enjoyed. He obviously shared many of the same ideals they Reveres held dear: the highest moral character, trustworthiness and honesty; making an excellent product; and providing the very best service to clients. Of course, he had generals over the foundry works who he trusted completely:

Henry Northey Hooper, 1843. *From public domain.*

Thomas Richardson, William Blake and John W. Sullivan, among others. When considering the entirety of the Hooper era after the Reveres, these were the men who really knew how to make excellent bells while Hooper "minded the store." The reputation of the Revere name carried on after Hooper acquired the company, and he continued the tradition of excellence in every aspect of making fine bells and wares.

By all accounts, Hooper seemed to have cut a dashing and impressive figure in his day. He was a very striking man in appearance, with a steadfast countenance and dapper dress—complete with a top hat and cane, as depicted by Winslow Homer in his illustration for the May 26, 1860 edition of *Harper's Weekly*.

Although Hooper was so very dashing and successful, a mechanic and foundryman he was not. But there is no doubt that he was very engaged and involved in the operations of the brass, bell and foundry works, making regular circuits and showing appreciation to his company of artisans, mechanics and foundrymen. Unfortunately, a great deal of information about the bell foundry is difficult to come by, due to the loss and scarcity of company records. What is known is that in 1821, Paul Revere III partnered with master mechanic and bell foundryman William Blake to form Revere and Blake. In 1823, they were joined by John W. Sullivan and Henry N. Hooper and formed Paul Revere and Company, with Hooper as the company agent. In 1825, the business name changed to Boston & Braintree and yet again to Boston Copper Company, until 1830, when Hooper partnered with William Blake and Thomas Richardson to form Henry N. Hooper and Company. An account from the April 3–June 26, 1909 issue of *Domestic Engineering: An Illustrated Weekly* stated, "Henry N. Hooper was the financial and ornamental head of the firm whose office was on the corner of Commercial and Cross Streets. He left the mechanical arrangements entirely with Mr. Blake and Deacon Richardson."

One would like to believe that when Hooper became the successor to the Revere business, the change of hands was pleasant and amicable. It wasn't. Around 1828–29, the company was truly struggling to manage

HISTORIC ALABAMA BELLS

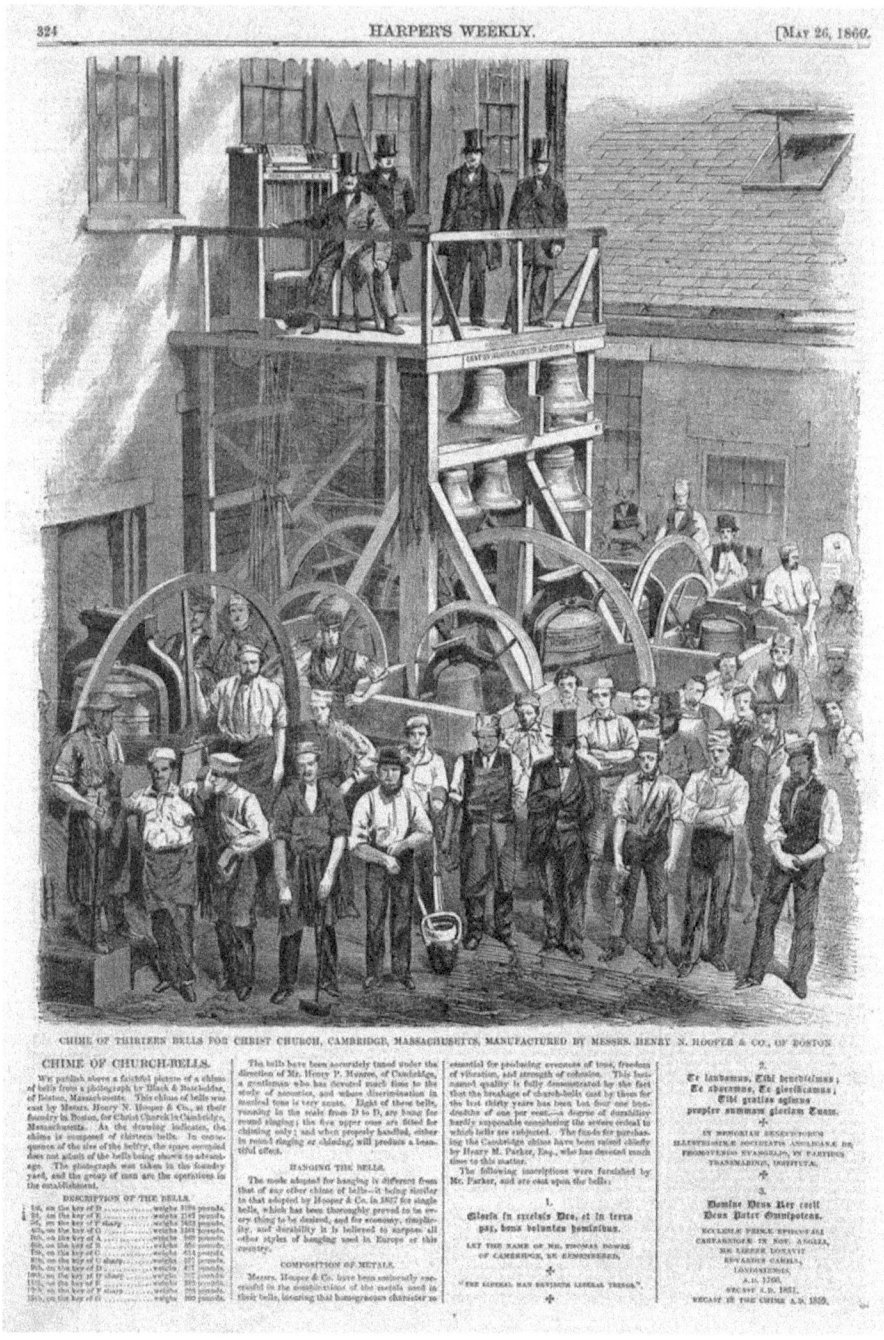

Winslow Homer's drawing of Henry N. Hooper and Company for the May 26, 1860 edition of *Harper's Weekly*. From public domain.

the business. It appeared that the foundry, including the Brass and Copperworks divisions, was in dire financial straits. The Reveres did not seem to have the resources to keep things running. Hooper, however, did have the wherewithal—or the potential capital with lending institutions—to keep the foundry works open and in business without any substantial losses. A complex and hard-fought legal battle ensued, and in the end, the entire operation went to Hooper. Still, Hooper had Blake and Richardson and the most extensive brass and bell foundry in the country. Because of its great reputation, the work continued on. Many great and wonderful bells were cast by the Henry N. Hooper Company in an unbroken continuity from the Revere tradition. Using the same physical facilities, methods, molds, materials and templates, they made bells that were among the finest instruments in America with their sweetly ringing peals, thanks to the skills of William Blake and many of the seasoned Revere and Son foundrymen.

It is believed that Hooper marketed the foundry's line of bell products to tower clockmakers, such as Edward Howard of Boston, for use as stationary clock bells. These were truly the integral components of striking tower clocks, which were evolving over time from being handmade to being industrially made—in step with the effects of the Industrial Revolution on America and Europe during the nineteenth century.

Henry N. Hooper carried on as the head of Henry N. Hooper Company until his death on September 19, 1865, in Roxbury, Massachusetts. His wife, Priscilla Langdon Harris Hooper, later joined him in death on June 25, 1884. Both are buried at Mount Auburn Cemetery in Cambridge, Massachusetts. Hooper's longtime partner and master artisan William Blake became the successor to Henry N. Hooper Company in 1868.

5
CAST BY HENRY N. HOOPER AND COMPANY, BOSTON

A Striking Tower Clock and Two Steeple Bells

The Alabama State Capitol Clock Bell: Montgomery, Alabama

In the early part of the nineteenth century, it became obvious that Alabama needed a permanent site for its state capital, which had traveled the locational circuits from the territorial capital of Saint Stephens; to Huntsville, upon achieving statehood; then to Cahawba, as the first permanent capital; then to Tuscaloosa when riparian flooding in Cahawba necessitated relocation. After much debate and deliberation, Alabama legislators finally voted in favor of moving the state capital to Montgomery in 1846. Montgomerians exuberantly and boastfully promised a capitol building of excellence, and they, indeed, delivered one that was very stately and opulent—a very fitting design by Philadelphia architect Stephen Decatur Button to crown a great southern state. Completed in 1847, no expense was spared in realizing the grand edifice, and from all accounts, a public timepiece was not part of the design. Two years of adulation over this example of architectural finery passed until fire broke out in the building on December 14, 1849, destroying everything except the foundation.

Shortly after the second, and present, capitol was built on the surviving foundation of the Stephen Decatur Button design, the citizens of Montgomery wanted to have a town clock that everyone could see, hear and tell time by, as there was no prominent public clock that fit the bill in the downtown at that time. Montgomerians eyed the top of the capitol

The 1847 capitol in Montgomery burning to its foundations. *From Alabama Department of Archives and History.*

portico pediment as the perfect place for a city clock and petitioned the state government for their request. This resulted in a joint resolution of the legislature on February 9, 1852, for approval by the City of Montgomery to place a town clock atop the capitol.

Following legislative approval, the City of Montgomery ordered a striking tower clock from Howard and Davis of Boston (later famously known as the E. Howard Watch and Clock Company) and installed the clock symmetrically atop the capitol's columned portico. Leaving the clock mechanism within its original wooden crate, they built the beautiful New England–style "aedicule" clock housing detail around it with huge black clock dials and contrasting white Roman numeral clock letters.

The Alabama State Capitol is the only extant state capitol in the United States with a striking tower clock as its most prominent architectural feature. There are many other reasons why the capitol is unique and highly significant as a historical icon, and yet, for whatever reason, the striking tower clock and bell have never been a high-profile research subject in the annals of the capitol's history narrative. This is indeed a curiosity; perhaps it is simply taken for granted as a reliable component of a building's makeup, much as

The 1851, and present, state capitol. *From the author.*

Clock *aedicule* atop the capitol and its stationary clock bell. *From the author.*

The massive 1850 Henry N. Hooper clock bell atop the capitol. *From the author.*

we think of modern lighting, mechanical, or electrical systems—we know they are there and working for us all the time. When these systems don't work, we immediately take notice and scramble to get things up and running again. Would that this level of urgency and care were true for antique tower clocks and historic bells!

Some see the art and science of making clocks and casting bells as archaic. They think they are outdated relics that have no place in the modern world.

What a tragic mindset! This should serve to heighten our awareness to preserve these special artifacts at all costs. These antique clocks and bells are marvels of invention and precision.

The Howard and Davis striking tower clock in the state capitol was engineered to mechanically and perfunctorily strike the hour on a tower bell, and in this case, it wasn't just any bell. It was a bell with an authentic connection to Paul Revere. Around the bell crown, the block letter inscription tells the exciting news we are looking for in our quest to understand how this bell is connected to Paul Revere:

Cast by Henry N. Hooper and Company, Boston 1850

Hooper was, as we have already learned, the longtime Revere & Son company agent who became the foundry's first successor in 1828. This bell was cast under the aegis of master bellcaster William Blake in the very same Revere bell foundry, using the same templates, molds and processes the Reveres had been using since 1792.

There is something of a mystery about the installation date of the state capitol clock and bell. The legislation enabling the City of Montgomery to place the clock atop the capitol portico was passed in 1852, and the Howard and Davis striking tower clock is estimated to have been cast circa 1854, but the clock bell was cast in 1850, during the time of the reconstruction of the present capitol and well before the legislation of 1852 that approved the city's gift of the clock to the capitol. Even more interesting, intriguing and confusing was speculation on the part of some that the clock and the clock bell were installed atop the capitol in 1859. We may never know the exact year for certain.

Inscription of the Hooper bell. *From the author.*

Before the clock was electrified, it depended on gravity to work. Through the use of heavy weights, which were wound weekly by the clock keeper, the pendulum and gears kept time. It has been proposed by an authoritative source that the capitol clock's weights are still within the walls because the clock's weight cables are still in the attic of the capitol and are taut. It is very likely that the weights may still be suspended in their chutes, or the cables were simply tied off for no obvious purpose. The outcome of this proposed existing condition remains to be seen.

Typically, when striking tower clocks were ordered, clock makers would partner with a bell foundry to obtain a stationary clock bell of their specifications and liking. Given that E. Howard and Davis Clock Makers were located in Boston and obviously knew the Henry N. Hooper and Company bell foundry, it was only natural and fitting that its standards of excellence matched those of the Hooper firm and that a Hooper clock bell would accompany an order for a striking tower clock made by E. Howard and Davis.

The mystery of the bell's casting date preceding the idea and legislative approval for a town clock is curious. It seems that perhaps the bell was cast for another client and, due to unhappy circumstances, could not be employed for use. Another possibility, which is quite plausible, is that the bell was cast as part of a prize-winning chime stand for the Massachusetts Charitable Mechanics Association Exposition of 1850. In the northeastern United States, where the early Howard and Davis striking tower clocks are more numerous, pairings with the Hooper Company for tower clocks seem consistent. One such example is the Jamaica Plain Unitarian Universalist Church in Jamaica Plain–Roxbury, Massachusetts, where the very same Howard and Davis striking tower clock was installed with a sizeable Hooper bell.

Howard and Davis striking tower clock, circa 1854, within the clock's *aedicule*. *From the author.*

The original clock's gravity-driven movement was replaced by electricity around the early to mid-twentieth century. *From the author.*

Until late 2014, the state capitol's Howard and Davis clock operated by the same electrification from the 1930s. The magnificent bell has been silent for the past few decades. However, if the clock and its stationary bell were authentically restored, they could become another high-profile point of interest of the state capitol's history, tradition and legacy, particularly since the capitol's Howard and Davis clock is estimated to be one of about twenty or so that have survived to our present day, as proposed by David W. Graf, master clockmaker and restoration artisan of Kittery Pointe, Maine. Graf was the restoration artisan for the Jamaica Plain Unitarian Universalist Church's striking tower clock. A former clock keeper for the capitol clock, who was familiar with the Liberty Bell, commented that the Hooper bell was approximately the same size as the nation's icon, and indeed it is. Weighing around a ton, when struck it could be heard up to three miles away from the capitol in a clear path across Montgomery.

At this writing, the Alabama State Capitol clock desperately needs to be venerated, honored and appreciated for its special historical significance,

The Jamaca Plain Unitarian-Universalist Church near Boston. *From Halley-Boston Creative Commons.*

The Jamaica Plain Unitarian-Universalist Church near Boston has an identical Howard and Davis striking tower clock, which has been restored to mint condition. *From Lawrence Zaborski.*

rarity and pricelessness as a unique and highly treasured artifact, particularly since it is the only one of its kind among all existing state capitols. In honor and celebration of our state's 200th birthday, let us pause to reflect on the fact that no other state capitol maintains the status of being a representative symbol as the birthplace of both the Civil War and the civil rights movement. It also enjoys a strong and meaningful connection to one of the outstanding and noteworthy figures of the American Revolution in Paul Revere, from whom we have inherited a tangible symbol of his legacy in the state capitol clock bell for all posterity.

Early Ramer Baptist Church, where the Hooper bell resides in the belfry. *From the author.*

THE SAMPEY MEMORIAL BAPTIST CHURCH: RAMER, ALABAMA

Ramer Baptist Church (original spelled *Ramah*) was organized on July 11, 1857, with George Granberry McLendon installed as the first pastor of the congregation. The church was renamed Sampey Memorial Baptist Church in 1947 in memory of Dr. John R. Sampey, who spent his childhood in Ramer and later became the president of the Southern Baptist Theological Seminary in Louisville, Kentucky, from 1928 until 1942. Ramer Masonic Lodge No. 243 was organized on June 15, 1857, and shared the second floor of the church building.

The discovery of this bell is a most interesting one. I was presenting a lecture on the rare and historic bell belonging to the neighboring Ramer United Methodist Church during its Summer Homecoming Day. Afterward, the pastor of the Sampey Memorial Baptist Church, Reverend Robert McMicken, who was in attendance, asked me to look at the church bell to see what kind of bell they had in the tower of their historic church. I agreed to take a look in the near future, but interest and curiosity about what was up in that tower got the best of members of the church, and they

Left: The 1859 Henry N. Hooper bell of the earlier Ramer Baptist Church building. *From Mike Mosely.*

Below: The Gainesville Presbyterian Church in Gainesville, Alabama, where the first bell was an 1839 casting by Henry N. Hooper Company. *From the author.*

climbed into the tower to look over the bell. They e-mailed me to share what they had discovered: a very rare Henry N. Hooper and Company bell cast in 1859! How unlikely and unique that a bell cast by Henry N. Hooper and Company should find its way into this small Alabama hamlet deep in the broad open space of south Montgomery County. It's even more surprising that it still remains in the steeple of this adaptation of a

New England meetinghouse. Ramer, Alabama, is a special place for rare and historic church bells. The history of how the bells came to Ramer is an unsolved mystery but a remarkable and outstanding story all the same!

THE GAINESVILLE PRESBYTERIAN CHURCH BELL: GAINESVILLE, ALABAMA

The Gainesville Presbyterian Church was organized on April 1, 1837, in this quaintest town in west Alabama. The founders of Gainesville were from New England, as evidenced by the architectural style of the Presbyterian and Methodist churches built there. The very first bell in the tower of the Presbyterian church was cast in 1839 by Henry N. Hooper and Company, and it lasted until March 8, 1880, when it cracked while tolling for a prominent gentleman named Mr. Bliss who had recently passed.

The 870-pound Hooper bell was sent back to the same Revere-Hooper foundry, which was now known as the Blake Bell Foundry, as Mr. William Blake succeeded Hooper upon his death. The old bell was accounted with credit toward a new 1,000-pound bell that the church had ordered as its replacement. The replacement bell by Blake was reportedly cast with silver dollars for a "sweeter sound." The Gainesville Presbyterian Church is one of the few churches in Alabama to have had two Revere-legacy bells from different periods in the bell foundry's history. Without a doubt, the Hooper bell belongs to the first decade of bells cast by Hooper after acquiring the foundry from the Reveres. Newspaper accounts of the first bell recall a bell with a very sweet sound. One of the most interesting parts of the story is how the church remained a loyal customer to the foundry forty-one years later, requesting a Blake bell of an even larger size, which you shall see shortly.

The 1839 Hooper bell weighed 870 pounds and served the church for forty-one years, until it cracked and had to be taken down and replaced. *Sketch by the author.*

6

WILLIAM BLAKE

Master Bell Caster for the Revere Bell Foundry

Of all the personnel associated with the Revere—subsequently Hooper—bell foundry, no name besides those two emerges from the company ranks as high as that of William Blake, the extremely able mechanic and master bell caster extraordinaire, and the man with the musical gift and ear. William Blake was all of these and much more. If Hooper was the man who could sell the Revere bells, Blake was the man who made Hooper's work so easy and natural because he made an excellent bell in every way—particularly with respect to full, rich and clear sound. This set the Revere bells apart from the early castings done by Paul Revere when he undertook bellmaking as a new supplemental enterprise of his copperwork.

To his great credit, Blake takes his place in history, together with his son after his death, as the second and last successor of the Revere bell foundry after Henry N. Hooper. He was the last owner until it closed under his son's tenure. Not much is known about William Blake, at least not yet. But we do have some insight about him from what is known about the success of the Revere bell foundry and its bells; how respected, prized and coveted they were; and who bought and installed them in their towers, steeples and cupolas. All of this would not have been possible were it not for a true master artisan being at work very quietly behind the scenes, training the apprentices to strive for excellence in the craft. Somehow, the picture of Blake at work in the furnace of the foundry is of a person with much patience and great forbearance, thoughtfulness and care for those working under him. Of course, this is conjecture, but we do have a couple of sources

William Blake may be the gentleman in the center, to the left of Hooper, in this Winslow Homer drawing for the May 26, 1860 edition of *Harper's Weekly*. *From public domain.*

who provide some clue as to his general manner and disposition. He did not seem to be a driver or pusher but a true artist whose work was finished when it was finished. This probably exacerbated the company foremen and superintendents, but it seems to be true of his entire life—unchanging until the end.

In an issue of *Domestic Engineering* from April 3–June 26, 1909, in an article titled "In Early Days—XXI," Herbert S. Renton reminisces about his father's employment with the Henry N. Hooper and Company and impressions of William Blake while in partnership with Hooper. Renton cites the location of the foundry in 1909 as being on Causeway Street in Boston—where the railway terminal was located at that time. It was here that Paul Revere started his foundry in 1792 with sons Paul Jr. and Joseph Warren Revere. In the article, Renton's father said, "William Blake was perhaps the best authority on metals and the best all-around foundry man in the United States."

During the years between 1804 and 1820, the foundry's historical narrative is somewhat silent, with the exception being that George Holbrook, an apprentice of Paul Revere, was already casting bells during this time and is recognized by some as the first *de facto* successor to the Revere bell foundry. Some have speculated that Paul Revere's son Paul Jr. was in partnership casting bells with Holbrook, but this has never been fully corroborated. Based on evidence presented by Edward and Evelyn Stickney, it is a possibility. During this period, Paul Revere and his son Joseph Warren Revere were also trying their hand at casting cannons, and in 1811, Paul Revere cast his last bell. Paul Revere passed away in 1818, and son Paul Jr. passed in 1813, which is unfortunate as the greater glory of the bell foundry was yet to come.

In the December 1898 issue of the *Foundry*, journalist Sam Due wrote the "Early History of the Bell Business," which was an article that focused almost exclusively on the Revere/Hooper/Blake bell foundry and provides probably the most insight on the person and work of William Blake:

> *In 1820, Mr. William Blake, a young man, probably as thorough a mechanic as could be found in the City of Boston at that time, by some means was into business relations with grandson Paul Revere III…and they, commenced again the making of bells, but under what name, or whether in connection with any other business is unknown….How long Revere was associated with Mr. Blake is not on record, but in 1823 was formed the Boston Copper Company, with Mr. Blake at its' head, showing that they too saw something in the manufacture of copper attractive….In 1828, a co-partnership was formed between Henry N. Hooper, William Blake, and Thomas Richardson under the firm name of Henry N. Hooper & Company, and was continued under that style until 1869, the company being by far the most important of it's character in the country, making not only bells, which it shipped to all parts of the world, but metals of all kinds for ship's use, such as sheathing and spikes, lamps and fixtures for oil and gas, cannon for the United States Government, and most of the machine work for the Lighthouse Department….In all of this work, Mr. Blake was the mechanic whose ability enabled them to obtain this prominence, although, as is often the case, his name was obscured by that of his associate, whose duties were confined to the office and selling departments.*

By January 1869, the partnership of the Henry N. Hooper and Company was dissolved, as both Hooper and Richardson had already died, and their interests were already withdrawn. William Blake reorganized the company and formed a partnership with his son, William S. Blake. They continuing as William Blake and Company until 1890, when the name of the bell foundry was changed to Blake Bell Company. There are conflicting records concerning the actual year in which the Blakes passed away. William Blake, the father, is listed as having died in 1871 and 1873, while William S. Blake is listed as having passed away either in 1894 or 1897. Nonetheless, while it is certain that the Revere bell foundry legacy did truly end with the death of the Blakes, an alternate narrative suggests that during the early 1890s,

George H. Lane acquired the company and began relocating company operations, resulting in the subsequent demolition of the foundry. We cannot corroborate the exact chronology of the last days of the bell foundry for certain, due to the lack of records and documentation. But we may say that the acquisition and demolition of the foundry itself was the end of the Revere/Hooper/Blake bell foundry. This was the end of practically one hundred years of fine bellmaking in the United States, but they left behind a vast treasure-trove of beautifully crafted and sweet-sounding bells as a lasting repertoire.

7
CAST BY BLAKE BELL FOUNDRY

A Gift from Northern Friends—a Second Steeple Bell

The Thrasher Hall Bell: Tuskegee University

Originally known as the Science Building, Thrasher Hall, so named for the prolific New England journalist and friend of Booker T. Washington Max Bennett Thrasher, was the first building on Tuskegee University's campus, which was designed by architect Robert R. Taylor, the first African American to graduate from MIT in 1892, who was recruited by Booker T. Washington to be both an educator and campus architect at Tuskegee. He served faithfully until 1932, except for a very brief period at the turn of the century. The building's construction began in 1893 and took a number of years to be fully completed. The sophistication and finesse of Taylor's Beaux-Arts architectural education are showcased here. The result is a splendid composition. Though it has sadly been altered for the worse, it does still retain its classic form.

The story of the Thrasher Hall bell is a curious one. It does appear in historic photos, though it is barely visible—you can just see the headstock, rope-wheel and the crown of the bell. Cast in 1894 by the Blake Bell Foundry, it is related to Paul Revere's bells in that it was cast by the very last successor to the Revere-Hooper bell foundry legacy. At the time of this writing, there are no known records detailing the bell's procurement for the college, though the inscription on the waist of the bell reads, "A Gift From Northern Friends." It is very possible that this bell was among the last to be

The 1894 Blake bell today, mounted in front of Thrasher Hall at Tuskegee University. *From the author with permission of Tuskegee University.*

cast by the foundry before it was acquired by George Lane in the mid-1890s and sadly demolished, bringing a sad ending to one of the most historic bell foundries in the land.

THE GAINESVILLE PRESBYTERIAN CHURCH SECOND BELL: GAINESVILLE, ALABAMA

To paraphrase the *Livingston Journal* from Friday, March 19, 1880, around the time the Gainesville Presbyterian Church building was being erected, two parishioners placed an order for a church bell with Mr. John Tappan of Boston. Tappan ordered an 870-pound bronze bell for $700 from Henry N. Hooper and Company, Boston. Gainesville Presbyterian Church's first bell was cast by Henry N. Hooper in 1839 and served the congregation for more than forty years. It cracked during the funeral of Mr. Bliss and was removed from the tower by Mr. Kring on Monday, March 8, 1880, and shipped to the bell foundry.

The new bell was ordered to be one thousand pounds and in the key of A. It was to be shipped by schooner from Boston to Mobile—a trip that

Left: The 1880 Blake bell at the Gainesville Presbyterian Church. *From Katie McGough Smith.*

Below: The large wooden rope-wheel of the 1880 Blake bell at the Gainesville Presbyterian Church. *From Katie McGough Smith.*

was expected to take several weeks—but there was actually a much shorter delivery time. The new bell was delivered to the church, raised and hung in the tower very likely around Friday, March 26, of that same year, as the *Gainesville Reporter* account on Monday, March 29, 1880, reported that "the new bell called the congregation to worship for the first time, on Sunday last." March 8 through March 26 seems to be a very reasonable window of time—the better part of three weeks—for the foundry to process the order and deliver the new bell. Church lore states that the bell was cast with fifty silver dollars to sweeten its peal.

We are fortunate to learn about the Gainesville Presbyterian Church bells thanks to the McGough family of Gainesville. Margaret McGough was very gracious in taking time to tell me stories concerning the church, the church bell and the town of Gainesville. She also made arrangements for photographs of the Blake bell, the second, and present, bell from the Revere/Hooper/Blake foundry, which has hung in the steeple of this fine church since 1880. Mrs. McGough's daughter, Katie McGough Smith, braved the old steps of the tower and a swooping attack by the resident tower owl, which had claimed the tower as its domain due to one of the tower's louvers being damaged—that is, until Mr. McGough had the louver repaired, so the owl could return to its natural habitat, and the wonderful old Blake bell could ring again to call the congregation to worship.

8

JOHN WILBANK AND THE LIBERTY BELL

BELLMAKER FOR INDEPENDENCE HALL
AND THE MAN WHO SAVED THE LIBERTY BELL

*W*henever July 4, 1776, is discussed, many Americans have a mental picture of the Declaration of Independence being read in Philadelphia before jubilant crowds outside Independence Hall while the Liberty Bell is being rung wildly from the octagonal cupola of the upper portion of the clock tower of the building. With all of the fanfare and excitement of the moment, of course, this is the authentic account of that most momentous and greatest day in United States history, right? Well, not exactly. To truly gain an appreciation for the story the Liberty Bell, we need to understand how the Pennsylvania Statehouse became Independence Hall. And we need to understand the story of the towers, clocks and bells that were employed throughout its history. This leads us to the story of J. Wilbank, the bell caster for Independence Hall and the reluctant rescuer of the Liberty Bell.

We must remember that these events occurred under British rule, when so many products for everyday life came from England. Though there were "light industries" at this time, the colonists still relied on importing certain items. It is also true that whenever buildings were demolished for whatever reason, doors, windows and other elements were saved and reused in the new building. The concept of practicing sustainability was common with our nation's forefathers, so it's not actually a new idea.

The original building of the Pennsylvania Statehouse—the meeting place of the assembly—was begun in 1732, though it was not completed until 1848. It was then, and still is today, the essential greater body of the present Independence Hall. Minus the current massive tower, it had a central cupola and front and rear balustrades. The old statehouse in Dover, Delaware, is an excellent model to visualize how the early Pennsylvania statehouse looked in terms of architectural type and appearance, though it is smaller in scale.

In 1750, the cupola was removed from the roof and a new steeple with a staircase and a belfry was erected, and in 1751, the assembly formally requisitioned a bell for the new tower.

Isaac Norris, speaker of the Pennsylvania Assembly, placed an order through the assembly's representative in London, Robert Charles, to procure a new bell for the statehouse from the Whitechapel Bell Foundry. It would contain an inscription from Leviticus 25:10, reading, "Proclaim liberty throughout all the land unto all the inhabitants thereof." Many historians believe this marked the fiftieth anniversary of William Penn's Charter of Privileges, which placed legislative power in the assembly rather than in the hands of William Penn and those who supported the Penn family.

Why the bell was dated 1852 instead of the year of the Charter (1851) has been a topic of debate, along with why Pennsylvania was misspelled. One of the most convincing and plausible explanations is that the bell would not arrive until late 1852, and the misspelling of the colony's name (Pensylvania) was because Isaac Norris was an opponent of the Penn family. Still, the bell arrived in port in late August or early September aboard Captain William

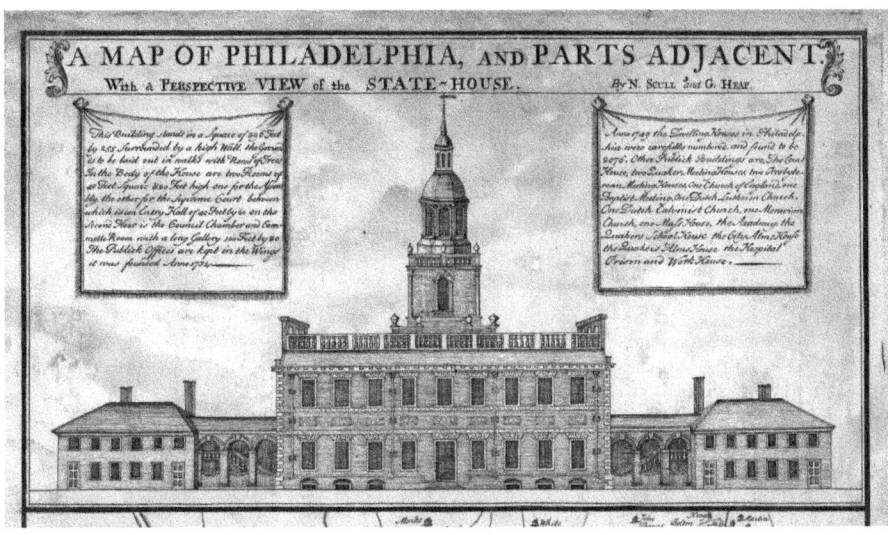

Independence Hall, 1752. *From public domain.*

The Bell's First Note 1753, by J.L.G. Ferris. *From public domain.*

Child's dry goods and passenger ship, *Hibernia*, which ferried cargo and passengers between the colonies, England and Ireland. On September 1, 1752, Isaac Norris wrote that "the bell is come ashore in good order....But we've not yet try'd the sound."

It was not until March 1753 that the new statehouse steeple was completed, and the new bell was hung to test the quality of the sound. In early March 1753, Norris wrote to assembly agent Robert Charles, "I gave information that our bell was generally liked and approved of, but in a few days after my writing I had the Mortification to hear that it was cracked by a stroke of the clapper without any other violence as it was hung up to try the sound."

It was at this time that Philadelphia ironsmiths John Pass and John Stow learned about the bell's fate to be sent back to Whitechapel Bell Foundry in London for recasting, and they presented a proposal to the assembly to recast the bell in Philadelphia at their foundry—which they did. In June 1753, the great bell was again raised in the new statehouse steeple and rung to test the instrument to the dismay of those, including Isaac Norris, who wanted to return the bell to England for recasting. Agent Robert Charles placed an order for a new bell from the Whitechapel Bell Foundry, and the assembly resolved to pay for the new bell while keeping the Pass and

Stow bell. However, when the new bell arrived and was tested, there was a consensus that it did not sound any better than the Pass and Stow bell. The Pass and Stow bell remained in the statehouse steeple to ring out for special occasions, and the new Whitechapel bell was designated as the statehouse clock bell and was placed in a turret on the roof in connection with the clock.

In the early to mid-1770s, the steeple built by Edmund Wooley in 1753 began to show signs of deterioration and damage. There were real concerns about ringing the great statehouse bell, and in historical narratives, it appears that the bell was more or less silent during this time. Even to this day, there is a controversy about whether or not the Liberty Bell rang on July 4 or on July 8, 1776, to announce and celebrate the Declaration of Independence. Due to the condition of the tower, it has been suggested that it may not have rung at all. Though the declaration was dated July 4, it took until July 8 to make prints to proclaim the Declaration of Independence publicly.

On July 8, 1776, it was read by Colonel John Nixon. The mighty throng went wild in the streets and beyond upon hearing the declaration, and the historical narrative states that all of the bells in the city were ringing upon this public proclamation of liberty, freedom and independence from England. It is difficult to imagine that some of the wild crowd did not climb the tower of the old statehouse and begin ringing that mighty bell.

By the same token, there is a plausible argument for asserting that the bell did not ring out that day, but that is a difficult proposal to accept, especially for an insane crowd that is beginning to fully grasp just what all of this meant in the moment. The written account states that "all of the bells in the city rang," and though the old statehouse bell is not mentioned specifically, I am satisfied that it did ring out gloriously in celebration of the grand declaration on that most eventful day—July 8, 1776.

In 1781, five years after the first public proclamation of the Declaration of Independence, the wooden portion of the steeple was removed, necessitating the lowering of the old statehouse bell to the brick chamber below its original station in the tower to the fourth floor. It was covered by a new, but less aesthetically pleasing, hip roof with an extruding finial detail. The original wooden steeple had been a concern for quite a while, and now that it was gone, fears of collapse, harm or injury were allayed.

In 1821, the two City Councils of Philadelphia procured a new bell for the statehouse's striking tower clock, which provided service until 1828, when the City Council of Philadelphia mandated that the statehouse steeple should be renovated and rebuilt. Philadelphia architect William Strickland was retained as the architect of the project. Strickland deviated from the

Back of the State House, by W. Birch, circa 1800. *From Library of Congress.*

original design by creating a tower clock and additional ornamentation. The city council also requested that the old statehouse clock, which was originally executed and installed by clockmaker Thomas Stretch in 1753, be replaced with a new tower clock and bell in the newly constructed steeple designed by William Strickland.

At this juncture in the historical account, we meet Philadelphia bellmaker John Wilbank, the reluctant hero who saved the Liberty Bell for future generations.

In 1828, the City of Philadelphia contracted John Wilbank, or the J. Wilbank Bell Foundry, to cast the new bell for the steeple, which would take the place of the old statehouse bell. This bell, not yet known as the Liberty Bell, was to be removed from the tower and hauled away for $400. In its place in the steeple would hang the new four-thousand-pound bell that John Wilbank had cast in December 1828. Upon realizing that the city's payment of $400 would not cover his costs of drayage for removing and hauling the bell away, Wilbank simply moved the bell to a different part of the tower.

Independence Hall. *From public domain.*

The 1821 clock bell also seems to have been removed during this time. It is believed that Wilbank took this bell as part of his payment. Wilbank was sued by the city for breach of contract, and in court, he countered that the drayage costs of removing and hauling the bell away exceeded the city's assessed value of the bell. Most interestingly, at some point, Wilbank was observed as beginning to realize how invaluable the bell was, and he began to see the great bell in a new light. He even expressed how important the bell and its legacy would be to future generations. Indeed, Wilbank's private inclinations were realized through an unexpected outcome. The city fought against Wilbank with its refutations and rebuttals until the judge ordered a compromise: John Wilbank would pay the court costs and the City of Philadelphia would keep the old statehouse bell, but it would still be Wilbank's bell on loan to the City of Philadelphia!

Over the years, and even in more recent times, ownership of the bell has continued to be a source of contention between the City of Philadelphia and the descendants of John Wilbank. But the Liberty Bell remains in the care of the National Park Service, which truly has the bell's best interests at heart for posterity, so future generations will appreciate this most valuable American symbol of all that is dear to us as a nation and a people. It is a resounding fact that the Liberty Bell was the very first artifact of United States history that was so outwardly symbolic of all that is promised and guaranteed in the Constitution to every U.S. citizen. In the mid-nineteenth century, it was embraced by African Americans in their quest for the same civil rights and liberties enjoyed by other citizens, even becoming the symbol and namesake of a heralded American abolitionist literature magazine that was published from 1839 to 1858. For all Americans, and to people worldwide, the Liberty Bell has been, and remains, the Morningstar of Freedom and Liberty.

9
CAST BY J. WILBANK

The Greensboro Presbyterian Church Bell

After saving the Liberty Bell in 1828, and well before it became known as one of our most important national treasures, John Wilbank simply carried on with his work. Foundry records and records of personal information are scarce—bits and pieces are known about him, but the overall impression of him seems to be that he was a serious-minded man of firm resolve and disposition. Very likely, he did not suffer fools gladly and took his art and craft very earnestly, accepting excellence as the only standard in all commissions he undertook. It seems that his motto after the unpleasantness of the lawsuit over the Liberty Bell incident was to press forward, which he did by carrying on his work of casting excellent bells and, along the way, employing a young apprentice who would figure greatly in the Wilbank Bell Foundry and the old Pennsylvania Statehouse: Joseph Bernhard.

The First Presbyterian Church of Greensboro, Alabama, or Greensboro Presbyterian Church, as it is most commonly known, was organized in 1823 by South Carolina pastor James Hillhouse, along with Revolutionary War veterans Patrick Norris and William Hillhouse, who were also church elders, or members of the church Session. The congregation erected a wooden building as its first house of worship around 1825 and built a new building out of brick in 1841, under the pastorate of the Reverend Thomas Sydenham Witherspoon. The church was likely outgrowing its facilities after the first thirty-four years, which resulted in the construction of the third, and present, church structure in 1859, under the tenure of the Reverend J.C.

The First Presbyterian Church with the Wilbank church bell in Greensboro, Alabama. *From the author.*

Mitchell. Made with a number of the handmade bricks reclaimed from the 1841 church building, the present house of worship was designed and built in the style influenced by the celebrated nineteenth-century architect Ithiel Town. This notable American architect is credited with bringing Gothic Revival architecture to the United States with his design for Trinity on the Green Episcopal Church in New Haven, Connecticut. The 1859 brick church in Greensboro is remarkably similar in architectural character, except for the later steeple modification. It is also similar to the First Presbyterian Church of Montgomery, which very likely had connections, whether direct or indirect, to Ithiel Town. It was built by Montgomerian John Godwin and ably assisted in great part by the renowned African American architect and builder Horace King.

There is no doubt that when the 1841 sanctuary was built, the idea of hanging a church bell was in the minds of the church leadership and building committee members, since the date of the church's construction and the date of the bell's casting are both from the same year. A bell was

Historic Alabama Bells

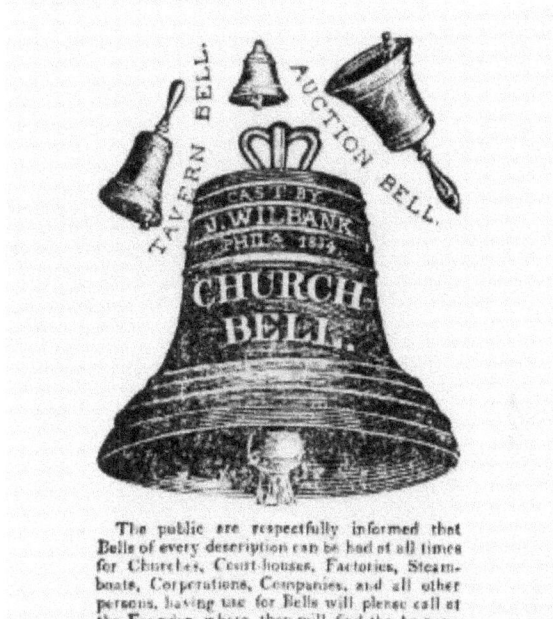

Right: Advertisement for J. Wilbank, circa 1830. *From public domain.*

Below: First Presbyterian Church in Greensboro, circa 1890. *From Alabama Department of Archives and History.*

Above: The 1841 J. Wilbank church bell in its mounting frame. *From the author.*

Opposite: Detail of the J. Wilbank inscription on the bell. *From the author.*

not in any way an express item. It took time to place, process and deliver an order, and it took time to hang it in the church's bell tower, usually with a team of horses or mules.

Almost all of the reputable bell foundries were located in the northeastern United States at the time, and the choice of a bell foundry was likely based on someone who was from the locality of a foundry, traveled there on business or knew someone who was acquainted with the foundry, its reputation and service. Many times, there was also a friend, relative or

member of another church who had procured a bell from a certain foundry and was very happy with it.

Thirteen years after John Wilbank saved the Liberty Bell and hung his large bell in the tower of Independence Hall, the First Presbyterian Church very likely called on Wilbank to cast a church bell for its new sanctuary. Due to the scarcity of church records that would provide more details about the church's business relationship with John Wilbank and the bell he cast for it, we can only attempt a plausible and educated guess about what may have transpired. The church leadership intended to have a bell in the tower for the day of dedication, which would be the very first worship service held in the new sanctuary. There was obviously funding for such a bell, and one or more members obviously knew of the Wilbank name and reputation—despite the controversy over the Liberty Bell. That the government requested Wilbank's services in the first place spoke volumes about his reputation as a bellmaker, since at that time, the Meneelys, Reveres and Holbrooks were in full force and were known as excellent bellmakers. The First Presbyterian Church of Greensboro made a wise choice in selecting Wilbank to make a bell for the beautiful new church in 1841. It certainly did not realize that its choice would be such a historic one for its congregation 178 years later, when Alabama celebrated its 200th birthday.

The Wilbank bells are marked by what is known as a "German Lip," which is more of a sheer detail from the bell's waist to the mouth of the bell. This is unlike the English tradition of bell casting, which features a curved profile to the bell's mouth. The German Lip could be thought of as a half-cyma-fillet detail, while the English bells have a definitive cyma form from the bell waist to the bell mouth. Proportional reeds act like visual scoring lines, bringing an aesthetic grace and beauty to the casting, while at the same time defining the bell's shoulder, waist, sound bow and lip.

It is quite obvious that John Wilbank was the maker of this bell, and he was likely assisted by an apprentice—possibly John Bernhard, who was

The "German Lip" and crack on the bell. *From the author.*

employed in Wilbank's bell foundry and, in the years following the making of the Greensboro bell, succeeded Wilbank as foundry owner. Bernhard even had an opportunity, like Wilbank, to cast a much smaller bell for Independence Hall, which now resides at Villanova University.

The Wilbank bell that replaced the Liberty Bell in 1828 became the workhorse bell of Independence Hall, according to Robert Gianini III, museum curator, Independence National Historic Park. It was replaced by the massive Meneely and Kimberly Centennial Bell of 1876, which commemorated our nation's 100th birthday. Today, the 1828 Wilbank bell hangs in the tower of the William Strickland–designed city hall of Germantown, a historic district within the Greater Philadelphia area.

Wilbank bells are rare. At the time of this writing, the Greensboro Presbyterian Church bell is believed to be the only Wilbank bell in Alabama. How fortunate the First Presbyterian Church of Greensboro is to have such a treasure with ties to the man who saved the Liberty Bell from becoming scrap and who cast even more bells for Independence Hall. How wonderful for this beautiful church and city and for our great state to have this connection with one of the most important major icons of American history.

10

THE LIBERTY BELL IN ALABAMA

The Genuine Article and the Replica

*I*f one were to ask the average Alabamian if the Liberty Bell had traveled beyond Independence Hall and Philadelphia to make stops for public viewing and official ceremonies, most would probably answer no—at least, in the days before the advent of the internet, which puts information at one's fingertips. And yet, this is exactly what happened in the great state of Alabama on the very first excursion of the Liberty Bell on a southbound journey to the World's Industrial and Cotton Centennial Exposition in New Orleans, Louisiana, in 1885. This was the first of seven journeys that the Liberty Bell made over a period of thirty years, before the decision was made to discontinue touring the bell due to concerns about further damage and harm because of the long travels by rail. Of course, tremendous care and precautions were taken to ensure that the bell would not suffer any further damage to its famous crack, but even so, it seemed that objections against touring the bell were loud, even during the first tour from Philadelphia to New Orleans.

In anticipation of the grand event, on November 19, 1884, New Orleans mayor J.V. Guillote wrote to William B. Smith, mayor of Philadelphia, requesting the loan of the Liberty Bell for the exposition. On December 23, 1884, the Philadelphia City Councils passed a resolution approving the loan of the Liberty Bell to the City of New Orleans and stating the terms of details for its safe passage to and from the event. Though the exposition started on December 16, arrangements were made for the bell to leave Philadelphia on January 23, 1885. It would pass through several states and

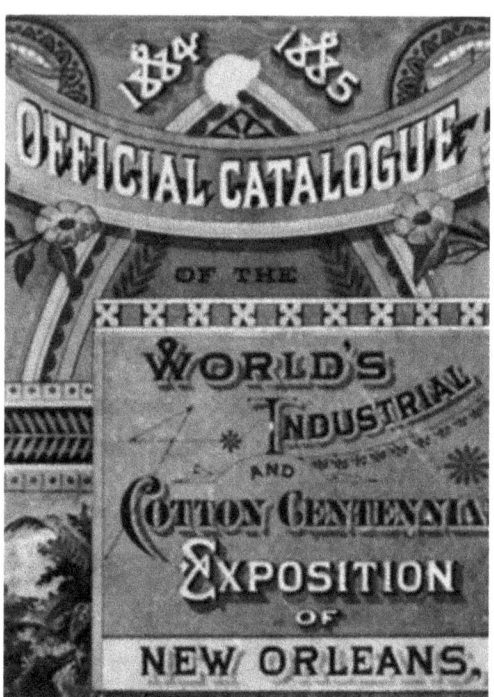

Leave Philadelphia, Friday, January 23d,	10.00 A. M.
Arrive Lancaster, Pa., " " "	12.00 M.
" Harrisburg, Pa., " " "	1.20 P. M.
" Altoona, Pa., " " "	5.00 P. M.
" Pittsburgh, Pa., " " "	9.50 P. M.
" Columbus, O., Saturday, January 24th,	5.30 A. M.
" Cincinnati, O., " " "	10.30 A. M.
" Louisville, Ky., " " "	6.00 P. M.
" Nashville, Tenn., Sunday, January 25th,	8.00 A. M.
" Birmingham, Ala., " " "	3.00 P. M.
" Montgomery, Ala., " " "	6.00 P. M.
" Mobile, Ala., Monday, January 26th,	8.00 A. M.
" New Orleans, " " "	12.00 M.

Above: The Liberty Bell's special train car. *From public domain.*

Opposite, top left: The 1885 Philadelphia to New Orleans travel schedule of the Liberty Bell for the Centennial Exposition *From public domain.*

Opposite, top right: Poster for the 1885 Centennial Exposition. *From public domain.*

Opposite, bottom: The 1885 schedule of stops for the Liberty Bell. *From public domain.*

Weekly Iron Age article dated Thursday, January 29, 1885, reporting on the Liberty Bell's arrival in Birmingham. From Birmingham Public Library archives.

make scheduled stops in a number of cities along the way: Lancaster, Altoona and Pittsburgh, Pennsylvania; Columbus and Cincinnati, Ohio; Louisville, Kentucky; Nashville, Tennessee; and finally, Birmingham, Montgomery and Mobile, Alabama.

The Liberty Bell's travels were tremendously covered by the press during all of its excursions, and that was no less in Alabama. One account that captures the spirit of the moment quite well was in one of Birmingham's early newspapers, known as the *Birmingham Iron Age* (later the *Weekly Iron Age*). The article was published on Thursday, January 29, and reported the bell's stop in Birmingham on Sunday, January 25, where a crowd of two thousand people was on hand to celebrate and venerate this national icon's visit to the city. The celebration included honorable dignitaries, a formal ceremony and no lack of pomp and show. The special train ferrying the Liberty Bell pulled into the Birmingham Terminal at half-past four to a packed station. The crowd occupied every available space and even climbed to the roofs of the parked freight cars in the trainyard at the foot of Nineteenth Street to get every seat in the house to see this glorious old bell.

Mayor Alexander Oscar Lane, along with an unnamed reporter from the *Weekly Iron Age*, referred to in the article as the "Age Man," were permitted entrance into the special car carrying the Liberty Bell by the three policemen tasked with guarding the bell: Sergeant Edward Malin and Officers Thomas H. Newman and John Patton, who were members of the reserve corps of the City of Philadelphia Police Department. Incidentally, Mayor Lane was the editor of the *Iron Age* before becoming the mayor of Birmingham. Both Mayor Lane and the Age Man were presented with medals that were embossed with a replica of the Liberty Bell. These special medals would also be given away to visitors at the New Orleans Exposition.

"Let me touch the bell!" was the banshee cry heard everywhere as hands were extended toward the bell and children were lifted up to the guards

The Liberty Bell in its special mounting frame for the journey by rail. *From public domain.*

so that they might touch it. It was exuberant, highly charged, friendly pandemonium as policemen used all of their might to stave off being overcome by the pressing crowd. The *Weekly Iron Age* article described the rail as "built as a regular passenger coach, while the rear portion was open and surrounded by an iron railing, and here the bell was suspended from an arch, on which was inscribed: '1776 PROCLAIM LIBERTY.'" The car was named the "Pennsylvania," and on either side were the words "Philadelphia–New Orleans," with two clasping hands between.

After fifteen minutes passed, the Liberty Bell's special train car was relocated to the front of the Relay House, where the Honorable Joshua T. Owen, of the official escort, made a short speech to the crowd. He provided a brief history of the bell and shared,

> [The bell] *was brought south as a silent messenger of peace to speak as no orator could speak to the people of the South, and make them, as well as the people of the North, forget that they were ever soldiers in the late war: that he hoped it's* [sic] *advent here would hasten the day when the gray and blue shoulders should teach and all the people of our country would remember only that they live in one country and under one flag. He was glad to see so many young people in the audience, for when they were grown, they could look back and say with pride that they had seen the old Liberty Bell on its way to bring peace and good will to all men.*

Owen's speech, notably spoken in Birmingham in the era of the segregated South, some eighty years before the civil rights movement in America, actually became highly prophetic for African Americans. For former slaves, and descendants of former slaves, the Liberty Bell became a deeply beloved and significant symbol for the liberty, equality and freedoms the Constitution guaranteed—indeed, civil rights for every American citizen.

After Birmingham's grand reception, the train carrying the Liberty Bell moved on to toward its next destination—the capital city of Montgomery—for another grand reception, then on to the port city of Mobile for yet another grand reception, before the special train carrying the bell made the final leg of the journey to Biloxi, Mississippi, and finally New Orleans and the exposition.

One of the purposes for the loan and exhibition of the Liberty Bell was to heal the wounds between the North and South from the War Between the States twenty years earlier. Evidence of healing were clear, beginning with Mayor Guillote's warm and endearing letter to Mayor Smith. The healing was reinforced by the former president of the Confederacy, Jefferson Davis, when he spoke of the power of the bell to heal the nation's wounds in Biloxi: "Glorious Old Bell, the son of a revolutionary soldier bows in reverence before you."

The south face of the Alabama State Capitol and the Liberty Bell replica on the Avenue of Flags. *From the author.*

THE ALABAMA STATE CAPITOL REPLICA OF THE LIBERTY BELL

In 1950, during a campaign drive to sell savings bonds, every state and U.S. territory received a full-scale replica of the Liberty Bell cast by the Paccard Foundry of Annecy, France—a world-renowned bell foundry that had been casting bells since 1796. The Alabama State Capitol replica of the Liberty Bell is located on the south lawn at the center of the Avenue of Flags and on axis with the south entrance and the Department of Archives and History. The bell is practically an exact facsimile of the original—minus the iconic crack, of course—and weighs 2,080 pounds. All of the fifty carefully detailed replicas allow visitors and tourists to see what the Liberty Bell looked like

The Liberty Bell replica, cast by the Paccard Bell Foundry of France, on the South Lawn of the capitol, along the Avenue of Flags. *From the author.*

before developing its signature fracture. It also allows visitors an idea of how the Liberty Bell originally looked before its patina was polished away.

The Alabama Liberty Bell replica has now taken its place in history as a faithful recreation of our cherished national and historic symbol of liberty and freedom and serves as a wonderful artifact and teaching tool of our American and Alabama history for future generations.

11
THE CHURCH OF THE NATIVITY

FIRST BELL FOR THE CSA
AND SECOND BELL MADE OF STEEL

*I*n 1836, the congregation of the Church of the Nativity, Episcopal in Huntsville was seeking to organize. It was officially chartered six years later, in December 1842, and was so named because of the Christmas season. Parish life officially began in May 1843, when it was admitted to the Diocese of Alabama, and in 1845, the church purchased a lot to begin construction on the first church building. It was made of brick, and upon completion, the first service was held in August 1847.

The second building—the current main sanctuary—was designed by New York architects Wills and Dudley and was built beside the first sanctuary. It was completed in time to hold service on Easter Eve in 1859. The spire is 151 feet tall, and the edifice has a five-hundred-seat nave, aisles lighted by windows of tracery, an organ chamber and a vestry.

The original church was razed in 1878, and the second structure was known as the finest example of Gothic Revival architecture in the South and became a national historic landmark in 1992. The church's first bell was bronze and was purchased for $250, only to later become a committed member of the Confederate cause, as it was melted down in neighboring Mississippi for munitions.

The present bell, a half-ton steel bell cast by Naylor and Vickers of Sheffield, England, in 1865, replaced the previous bell that was lost to the Confederate war effort and faithfully serves the church to this very day. The Naylor and Vickers Bell Foundry gained a respected reputation for its unique casting of steel bells, which are found throughout the United Kingdom and

Left: The Church of the Nativity Episcopal Church in Huntsville, Alabama. *From the author.*

Right: The massive Naylor-Vickers steel bell of Nativity Episcopal Church, which was cast in 1865 in Sheffield, England. *From Elaine W. Hamner.*

beyond. One of the most famous of its cast steel bells is the Steel Monster of Clerkenwell—the tower bell of Saint Peter's Italian Church, which overlooks Hatton Garden on Clerkenwell Road in London. It is believed to be the largest steel bell in England. The Nativity bell, true to the standard of the Naylor and Vickers reputation, has a wonderful and powerful voice and can be heard from long distances. No longer a swing-ringing bell, it is now intoned by a hammer—in the same manner as Big Ben in London—and is a delight to hear in the surrounding Twickenham Historic District and downtown Huntsville.

12
FIRST PRESBYTERIAN CHURCH OF WETUMPKA

CHURCH BELL OFFERED TO THE CSA AND TURNED DOWN

Around the time of the founding of the town of Wetumpka in 1834, future congregation members were being gathered to form a new Presbyterian church, which was organized in 1836 by the Reverends Fields Bradshaw and Alexander Cunningham. The congregation met in a converted building in West Wetumpka, which was part of Autauga County at that time, according to Sharon Fox, curator of the Elmore County Museum in Wetumpka. In 1856, the church began to plan a new sanctuary in the Gothic style, with a budget of $2,300. In setting out to retain an architect to design the new building, the Reverend G.R. Foster's meeting with a Montgomery architect was deemed "unsuccessful."

A church member obtained a set of plans for a church from a Mr. Alley, who was known to be a local builder in the area. Adopting the plans from Mr. Alley, and making some changes to them, the construction of the sanctuary was underway in August 1856, and on June 14, 1857, the church was formally dedicated. In its original design and construction, the church was a wonderful expression of Neo-Gothic architecture, with vestiges of Belgic and Italian Gothic in the use of the decorative pinnacles, finials and spires.

The church has a deeply significant history in Alabama, as William Lowndes Yancey, the fiery orator and Voice of Secession who led to the dissolution of the Union and the War Between the States, and Governor Benjamin Fitzpatrick were members of this church. The Wetumpka Light Guard also departed for service with the Confederate army in 1861. One of Alabama's

Left: First Presbyterian Church in Wetumpka. *From the author.*

Right: Historic photograph of the First Presbyterian Church in Wetumpka as it appeared in its original design and form. *From the First Presbyterian Church, Wetumpka.*

most distinguished senators, who served in the Civil War as a captain for the Confederate army, was married in this church following the war.

Reflecting on the church history, the Reverend Jonathan Yarboro shared a memory of a long-deceased congregation member whose ancestor witnessed the team of horses raising the bell to its lofty heights as the church was being finished for its formal dedication in 1857—the same year the bell was made.

A most significant story from the church's history occurred on April 9, 1862, when the church congregation and members passed a resolution authorizing the church trustees to present the church bell to the Confederate States of America (CSA) or the governor of Alabama for the defense of the Confederacy. They did so by tendering a letter to the secretary of war in Richmond, Virginia, on April 11, 1862. On April 22, the Ordnance Office of the CSA replied to the congregation with thanks for the offer of the bell but requested that they hold the bell subject to order, as contributions and metal on hand were ample to supply the foundry furnaces for some time to come. Incredibly, the bell was never needed and survived the war.

Tragically, though the bell survived the war, the bell tower was heavily damaged many years later by a hurricane. This required a shortening

Historic Alabama Bells

Left: The historic 1857 Meneely West Troy church bell, which survived the Civil War, a hurricane and a devastating tornado. *From the author.*

Below: The inscription of the 1857 church bell. *From the author.*

of the tall tower to its longstanding height and form. More than a century later, tragedy struck again. On Saturday, January 19, 2019, an EF-2 tornado on a devastating path through Wetumpka shattered and totally destroyed the First Presbyterian Church and severely damaged the neighboring First Baptist Church. Much of the surrounding area in downtown Wetumpka was damaged, though thankfully and blessedly,

A before-and-after photo of the First Presbyterian Church, which was all but destroyed in the path of a tornado. *From the First Presbyterian Church, Wetumpka.*

no lives were lost in the disaster. When the tornado had passed and cleanup operations began, the site was scoured for items precious to the congregation. A number of these were found and recovered—including the historic church bell, which had crashed on its side as it fell with the steeple. When it was discovered and hoisted up and away from the carnage of timber that was once the steeple, its clapper struck a wonderful peal as if to say, "I'm here, and I'm all right."

The church was also able to salvage practically all of the mounting and assembly parts of the bell, though some were broken beyond repair and others were likely unreliable for future use due to the tremendous impact of the steeple hitting the ground. Still, these will likely be good for use in the church archives or as a future display. Most of all, the historic bell will be preserved by the church for posterity and will hang in the reconstructed church steeple and ring again for First Presbyterian and the Wetumpka Community for generations to come.

13
SAINT PAUL'S EPISCOPAL CHURCH

How a False Threat of Smallpox
Saved the Town and the Bell

*C*eded to the U.S. government by the Creek Indians, and first known as "McGill's Hill," a beautiful, long brow of a hill known as Lowndesboro Ridge that rolls down into the lowland areas of the Alabama River attracted a number of settlers around 1815, before Alabama became a territory or achieved the status of statehood. Anyone who has ever traveled through this part of Alabama knows it is simply one of the most beautiful places in the state, with great viewsheds in abundance. One can see why this was a dream for the families who moved here from Virginia and South Carolina.

As the area was eventually organized as Lowndes County in 1830, McGill's Hill was renamed Lowndesborough in honor of William Lowndes, the South Carolina congressman, though it was later shortened to the present spelling: Lowndesboro. In 1856, Lowndesboro became an incorporated town and a great plantation community as people began planting and growing cotton on the river lowlands, building their homes and houses of worship over the course of time.

Baptists, Methodists, Presbyterians and Episcopalians were the earliest denominations in the growing community, and each congregation grew and developed differently. They built houses of worship at different times, but they were all built beautifully in their own unique architectural expression.

Of these fine churches, Saint Paul's Episcopal Church radiantly shines as a tremendous example of Richard Upjohn's *Rural Architecture*, which was intended to help small congregations build houses of worship in the tradition of Gothic Revival. The only, and very capable, daughter of one

Above: The 1859 Jones and Company bell at Saint Paul's Episcopal Church in Lowndesboro. *From the author.*

Left: Saint Paul's Episcopal Church in Lowndesboro. *From the author.*

The bell at Saint Paul's Episcopal Church in Lowndesboro in its original mounting frame. *From the author.*

of the most prominent plantation owners in the state, Dorian Bonnell Hall, had grown up as a Baptist but later became an ardent Episcopalian and was the driving force—and likely one of the chief benefactors—in the church-building campaign. The Upjohn book, or an excerpt from it, was appealing to Mrs. Hall, very much the go-getter, who had been raised to manage the family plantation after her father's death. Her devotion to Saint Paul's Church, as it was known to most in shorthand, was no different, and it seems that the church was constructed on an efficient schedule, being completed in 1857.

The church's history says that the first church bell was ordered from England, and once it was cast and en route to the States, the ship sank with the bell in it. Of course, this necessitated an order for another bell, but this time it would come from one of the greatest U.S. bell foundries: Jones and Company of Troy, New York. In their day, Jones bells were highly regarded for their excellent sweetness of peal and tonal quality, even in the larger bells. Saint Paul's bell, cast in 1859, is evidence of this high standard in bellmaking and has endured the past 160 years extremely

The inscription of the name of the bell's donor on Saint Paul's bell. *From the author.*

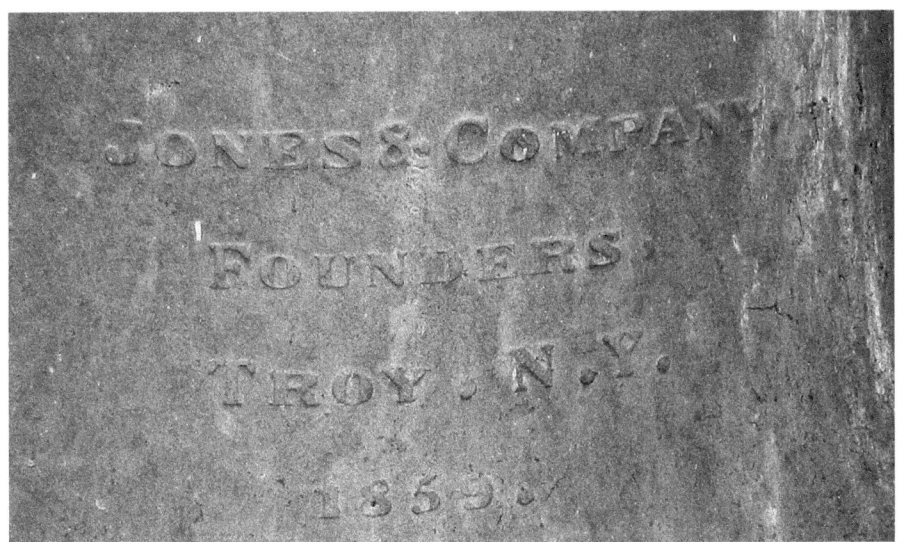

The bell founder's inscription on the Saint Paul's church bell. *From the author.*

well—even with respect to the instrument's hardware, mountings and wooden rope-wheel, which usually deteriorate the most over time.

The foundry inscription reads:

> *Jones and Company*
> *Founders*
> *Troy, N.Y.*
> *1859*

The donor's inscription reads:

> *Presented to Saint Paul's Church*
> *Lowndesboro, Alabama*
> *By Mrs. Dorian Hall*

Thankfully, the bell has survived in a very good state of preservation, given its age and use. But there was a moment in time when it appeared that not only the bell but the entire town of Lowndesboro would be threatened with complete devastation and destruction. During the last days of the Civil War, in April 1865, Union general James H. Wilson and his "Raiders" were heading into town when the town doctor went to where Wilson was camped, next to Rosewood Plantation. He convinced Wilson that there was an epidemic of smallpox in the town and warned him not to go into Lowndesboro. Wilson took this advice, which saved most of Lowndesboro, including the beloved and beautiful Saint Paul's Church—and its bell.

All because of a town doctor who told a "big one."

14
OLD FIRST PRESBYTERIAN CHURCH

The Church of the Leaders of Secession

As the leader of the South's secession from the Union and the founder of the Confederate States of America, William Lowndes Yancey, who was previously a member of the First Presbyterian Church of Wetumpka, served as an elder in one of Montgomery's most significant and oldest extant church buildings in the city—indeed, one of the earliest still standing in our state. The Old First Presbyterian Church on Adams Avenue was built in 1845 by Montgomery builder John P. Figh and the very noble and gifted Horace King—both of whom significantly contributed to the rebuilding of the Alabama State Capitol a few years later. The Montgomery County Historical Society's very own dwelling is John Figh's original late 1830s home, built by Figh himself, with help from Horace King.

Horace King enjoyed a tremendous reputation with John Godwin as a bridge builder before coming to Montgomery. He was known to draw upon the knowledge and expertise of another bridge builder, architect Ithiel Town, who was widely known in the early nineteenth century as a master engineer and bridge builder in addition to his exemplary practice of architecture. Town apprenticed under Asher Benjamin, another master architect, whose building pattern books were used by many early Americans, including architects in Alabama and the Deep South. With Godwin, King was said to have studied and employed Town's lattice truss designs for bridges, incorporating Town's convention into a number of his bridges built across the South.

Above: The Old First Presbyterian Church in Montgomery. *From the author.*

Left: Drawing of architect Ithiel Town. *From Trinity on the Green Episcopal Church, New Haven, Connecticut.*

Architect Horace King. *From public domain.*

It is not at all out of the question that both men became acquainted with Ithiel Town, but supposing that they did not, it is entirely logical that they were aware of and drew upon Town's design for the Trinity Church on the Green—the first Neo-Gothic church in the United States after the Gothic Revival in England—for this new Presbyterian church in Montgomery. A side-by-side comparison of Trinity Church on the Green and First Presbyterian leads to an astounding conclusion of architectural intention based on precedent. Trinity Church on the Green was designed circa 1813–15, and of course, First Presbyterian was built thirty years later, probably begun on paper before or around the time of Town's death in 1844 at age sixty. The fact that Godwin and King were using Town's intellectual property speaks to the very high probability that there was a relationship and exchange between the parties. Architects on both sides of the Atlantic during this time were very protective, jealous and territorial about their work and who should do it. Many architects wrote in trade journals about how carpenters and artisans were passing themselves off as architects and how wrong, unfair and injurious this was to the profession.

There is, though, a bit of a puzzling anomaly in the historical narrative. In Matthew Blue's coverage of events in 1847, the year the new, and present, church was dedicated, credit for the design was given to one Alexander McKenzie, a member of the church. Given that this is authenticated fact, pertaining to his involvement and authorship of the design, it is entirely possible that Blue may have misidentified Angus McKenzie, who was a ruling elder in the church during the exact time frame of the building period. Angus might have been centrally involved in the project as a committee chair, but only detailed records and minutes would give us the details needed to verify this hypothesis. If this were the case, it is possible that he met with Figh and King and provided them with a sketch of the plan and some idea of the desired look that the congregation wanted, which was based on Town's design in New Haven. McKenzie may have also known Ithiel Town. All of this is entirely possible.

Still, there are two factors that must be noted concerning McKenzie's credit as the architect of record. First, it is generally unusual for a member of a church to be the designer. In most instances, church leaders want outside, objective parties to design and build their edifices in the event of contractual disputes or issues deciding general matters of taste and aesthetics. Second, a McKenzie design of this caliber would not be an isolated event—there would be other commissions, and his name most assuredly would be found in the annals of historic nineteenth-century architecture. To date, the name of Alexander or Angus McKenzie is scarce and practically nonexistent in the history of Montgomery's architectural narrative.

Based on the drawing of Trinity Church, it is so very apparent that it is Ithiel Town's very own unique architectural design that appears again in the First Presbyterian Church building on Adam's Avenue. Though it was transliterated to become uniquely First Presbyterian's own expression, it was very likely authored by Town and was realized because of the plausibility of an established and longstanding Ithiel Town/John Godwin/Horace King acquaintance, which John Figh became privy to as he began working with King.

The possibility of Ithiel Town's direct involvement with the design of First Presbyterian cannot be ruled out, as discussion and planning for the new church was surely ongoing prior to his death in 1844, and construction began in 1845. Figh and King were present in the region during this time, and it is entirely possible that Town was consulted and may have mailed plans for the church design to them. Mailing plans to clients was a common practice in those days and was regularly done by Town's firm partner, the

Amos Doolittle engraving of Trinity Church on the Green, circa 1820. *From Trinity on the Green Episcopal Church, New Haven, Connecticut.*

renowned Alexander Jackson Davis, also known as A.J. Davis. Further study is needed to bring out additional details and to confirm actual events, but there is a very real connection with Ithiel Town at work in the realization of this rare, unique and beautiful church building.

One would think that given the church's obvious connection with Ithiel Town, John Figh and Horace King, the pinnacle of architectural and

The Old First Presbyterian Church, in Montgomery shows the architectural strains of the Ithiel Town design in New Haven. *From the author.*

HISTORIC ALABAMA BELLS

The second bell of Old First Presbyterian Church, which was cast by the Meneely West Troy Bell Foundry in 1881, according to Christy Anderson. An A-mount still in the tower verifies that there was a first bell. *From Mike Williams.*

historical significance could not be any higher, but there is a historic bell cast by Meneely and Company of West Troy, New York, in the tower of Old First. It corresponds to the foundry records of the Meneely Company in the recorded description as being made for the First Presbyterian Church, Montgomery, Alabama, and weighing sixteen hundred pounds. The only missing information in the foundry record is the date of casting, but a recent photograph confirms that the in-situ tower bell was cast in 1881. This is curious, given that the church was dedicated in 1847. However, the photograph shows a Meneely A-Stand belonging to another bell, likely from an earlier period or casting, corresponding to the date of the church's dedication or shortly thereafter. This could only mean that the bell presently in the tower is the second church bell that replaced a previous bell for reasons unknown and seems to corroborate the information found in the Meneely West Troy Foundry record.

The answer to the mystery of the first bell came from Christ Church Cathedral in Mobile, where the 1847 Meneely West Troy church bell's A-stand perfectly matches the one in the recent photograph, leaning on

Andrew Meneely, founder of the Meneely Bell Company, which would later become the Meneely West Troy Bell Foundry. *From public domain.*

the wall next to the window. The first Presbyterian Church bell from 1847 served the church until 1881, when the present bell replaced it for reasons unknown. Obviously, the Session of the First Presbyterian Church was very pleased with the Meneely name and brand, as they placed an order with the foundry for a second bell thirty-four years later.

The origins of the Meneely Bell Foundry are impressive, adding even more historical weight to old First in consideration of its historic and highly significant bell. Before he began his own bell foundry in 1826, Andrew Meneely apprenticed under master bell caster Julius Hanks, son of Colonel Benjamin Hanks, one of America's earliest bellmakers, who was said to be connected with Paul Revere by association and possibly through apprenticeship. Andrew Meneely married Philena Hanks, a cousin of Julius Hanks, and though the lineage is questioned by some scholars, there yet remains scholarly interest in the idea of a relation to Nancy Hanks, mother of President Abraham Lincoln.

It has been proposed that Meneely succeeded Julius Hanks by absorbing his foundry works over time. The Meneely Bell Foundry continued operations until 1952 in West Troy, now known as Watervliet, New York, and is known as the first Meneely bell foundry. The second Meneely bell foundry was the Clinton H. Meneely Bell Foundry of Troy, New York, which began operations around 1870. Clinton Meneely began operations when he couldn't come to terms with his brothers, Edwin and George, in the original West Troy foundry.

Given the church's impressive resume of historic and highly significant credentials based solely on its merit of design, personnel, materials and methods, including its historic tower bells, the fair city of Montgomery is very blessed and fortunate to have this amazing and excellent treasure of architecture. It is truly a rare and invaluable example from a tremendous period of American architecture, created by true masters of architecture, engineering, construction and bellmaking.

15
RAMER UNITED METHODIST CHURCH

A Rare Pre–Civil War Bell

        amer United Methodist Church was chartered in 1850 and was not the only Methodist church in the town known then as Athens. The town's name changed to Ramer when the U.S. Post Office began using zip code order of numbering postal stations. The first church building was a simple clapboard structure, in the character of local style, but it was based on the typical New England Meeting House. There are two recollections of the church, but they are varied slightly regarding the front entrance and the architectural character of the steeple. The second church building, which is the present building, was built at the intersection of Hobbie Road and Highway 94, and in 1990, it was remodeled to its existing architectural expression.

    The church possesses two paintings that depict the first wooden sanctuary. In both works of art, the steeple is located in the same position, but there is an open belfry in one interpretation and closed in another. The open belfry version depicts a swing-ringing bell in the steeple, and one could conclude that the same bell is within the enclosed belfry with louvers for sound transmission. This graphic historical narrative supports the idea that the church had a bell from the very earliest days of its charter, though little else is known presently. What follows is an account of how I became acquainted with Ramer United Methodist Church and the historic church bell, and how special the bell really is.

    One sunny afternoon in the spring of 2013, my son, Tommy, and I took a drive into the countryside of south Montgomery County, just to have some father-son time. There was no rhyme or reason as to where we would drive. We were just driving, talking and having fun while enjoying a cold soda. Taking the most obscure and scenic country roads away from the beaten path, we wound up in Ramer at the well-known T-intersection next to the Ramer United Methodist Church. Noticing the cupola atop the church over my left shoulder and seeing a silhouette of a dark shape in the tower, I quickly glanced to see if the dark shape was a common cast-iron, steel alloy bell before driving on, and it wasn't! I immediately noticed the bronze color and then the shape of the bell—a similar profile to the Liberty Bell!

I turned the car around, parked and got out. I looked at the bell from all sides and angles from the ground, trying to identify the casting. It defied the signature earmarking of all of the bells I had seen before. There was something really different about this one, and I just couldn't settle on whether it was a Meneely West Troy bell or a McShane bell. It was truly difficult to tell, and this one had some distinctive signature elements that I had not seen on any other bell so far. It was definitely a rare bell, but as to who made it, I really did not know.

When we returned home later that day, I contacted the church to inquire about the bell and to let them know that it appeared to be a unique bell. Pastor Cooper Stinson was very gracious and granted permission for me to go up on the roof and look at the bell, and I expressed my interest to schedule a time to do so in the near future. Before I could travel back to Ramer, however, it seemed that curiosity had gotten the better of the cat! Pastor Stinson ascended the roof to see just what all this was about and contacted me to share the results of his findings: the bell was cast by Jones and Company of Troy, New York, in 1859, and it had a number inscribed on its middle section that might have been the weight of the bell! When I heard this news, I was absolutely stunned. I was under the impression that rural churches were only able to afford cast iron–steel alloy bells, but this was truly a rarity, as there is such a limited number of Jones bells. At the time, this appeared to be the only Jones bell in Alabama, though there is a record of the First Presbyterian Church of Huntsville possessing a Jones bell in its church belfry before a raging storm damaged the tower and the bell was broken as a result. As the reader has already observed, there are, in fact, the two other Jones bells in Alabama presented in chapters one and twelve.

To witness the joy of the church upon realizing that the bell was rare was reward enough. They took my counsel very seriously to heart when I told

Ramer United Methodist Church today, with the cupola holding the rare Jones bell. *From the author.*

them to let it remain in the tower, to resist all offers to sell it and to never let even a bell vendor try to persuade them to polish or skin its beautiful patina, which is the great contributor and agent of much of its value.

This bell enjoys the great privilege of surviving the Civil War—of not being taken down and melted for bullets or cannons. How it came into the possession of the church is not known at the time of this writing, so it remains a mystery to be solved. The bell corresponds to the model of a depot bell in the annals of the Jones and Company catalogues, so perhaps it was hanging in the train depot at Ramer or elsewhere. When rung, the bell has an amplified, sweet and clear voice. It is one of the best-sounding bells I believe I have ever come across.

The most common story regarding procurement of bells for churches is that there was a benefactor in the church who wanted to make a gift of a bell, or bells, to the church, and this could quite possibly be the case here. We learned earlier that the former Ramer Baptist Church—about two or three hundred yards away—has a Henry N. Hooper and Company bell from 1859—this same year as this Jones bell. This proximity is an astounding coincidence so far south of their makers. There are many loose threads surrounding these bells. Many questions remain as to how the Ramer United Methodist Church came in possession of it and the interest and connections to the Jones and Company Foundry.

The 1859 Jones and Company Bell, and son Tommy seen behind the bell. *From the author.*

Upshot of the front side of the 1859 Jones and Company Bell. *From the author.*

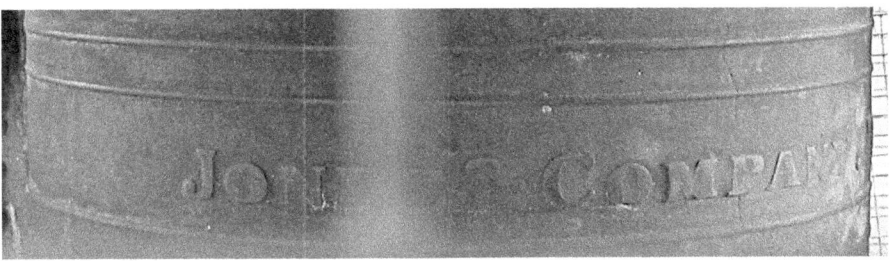

Inscription of the 1859 Jones and Company Bell. *From the author.*

There may yet be other Jones bells awaiting discovery in other Alabama steeples and towers, but not many more it would seem. Bells also turn up in other places, such as barns, attics, basements, abandoned ruins, historic structures, rivers, bays and lakes. Given the history of riverboats and steamships that were sunk while plying the rivers of our state, the Gulf of Mexico and Mobile Bay, there would have to be many more bells in the depths of these waters. Thankfully, the 1859 Jones and Company bell isn't one of them. How fortunate and blessed the Ramer United Methodist Church is in having such a prized bell as part of its history and heritage.

16
MAPLESVILLE BAPTIST CHURCH

A Bell Likely from Old Cahawba
and a Civil War Survivor

For those who enjoy doing detective work, what is both fun and frustrating at the same time is a case in which you cannot point to anything tangible as a clue, but you earnestly want to crack the case and solve the mystery. At the same time, you know that there is something authentic about the subject of your investigation, but before you can make a definite pronouncement, you need the facts. Such is the case of the bell of the Maplesville Baptist Church. Legend says that the bell came from the Methodist church in Old Cahawba, which was built in 1849. When the church ceased having services there, the bell was given to an African American church near Cahawba. The story goes that the bell fell from where it was hung in the church and was broken but was repaired by Kehn's Bell Service of Troy, New York. Eventually, the bell came into the hands of a trader who sold it to Mr. Thomas Ulmer Crompton, one of the founders of the Maplesville Baptist Church, who had it hung in the tower of the original 1907 church. The legend contains elements of believability but needs further research and study to establish the proven historical record. When the congregation built a new structure in 1960, the old bell was rehung in the steeple of the new sanctuary, where it still resides today.

Maplesville Baptist Church does possess a historic bell, and a highly significant one at that. Since it was cast in 1859, it survived the Civil War, though it could have easily been used as a spoil to be melted down and made into ordnance and munitions. Upon examination in the church steeple, there

The 1907 Maplesville Baptist Church—a beautiful expression of Vernacular architecture with Gothic accents. From *Clem Clapp.*

The Maplesville Baptist church bell, cast by Meneely West Troy in 1859. *From public domain.*

are some interesting elements of note about the bell. A Meneely West Troy bell cast in the decade of its making would be installed with the standard mountings and rope-wheel from the foundry itself, which were tremendous issues of pride with the bellfounders.

The Maplesville bell is missing its foundry-cast A-Stands, or A-Mounts, as well as the wooden rope-wheel made by Meneely. Instead, the bell is mounted into a pair of decorative cast-iron scrolls—a type of mounting that was cast by bellmakers such as G.W. Coffin, A. Fulton and a few others. Also, this bell contains several scoring lines around its waist, as though it were being prepared for inscribing the names of generous benefactors or a meaningful verse or quotation. Additionally, the clapper does not appear to be a Meneely West Troy clapper but from somewhere else, perhaps a local blacksmith's shop from that era.

Still, the bell is in excellent condition and has a wonderful patina. These are the factual aspects of the bell and cannot be disputed—the evidence is empirical. So, what does all of this mean with respect to the bell's history? No doubt this bell was once hung somewhere else with its original hardware and mountings. At some point in its history, it was either taken down or fell from where it was hung (which tracks with the legend) and then was salvaged for sale. In many cases, when bells are resold, they are together with the yoke still intact and without the other pieces of the hardware, or they are simply bare as a casting only. The only element that seems out of place is the mention of the Kehn Bell Service repairing the bell. The Kehn Bell Service was the successor to the Clinton H. Meneely Bell Company and was in business from the mid- to late twentieth century in Troy, New York. The two could have been conflated, especially if the narrative was being recounted around the threshold of the change in company hands. It is entirely possible that Clinton H. Meneely did repair the bell after its fall, which seems to place that event after the Civil War, when Clinton H. Meneely began his bell foundry with George H. Kimberly in 1870 because of a feud with his brothers over becoming a partner in their deceased father's foundry.

How fortunate is the Maplesville Baptist Church to have such a fine bell, even if there is still a need to continue researching, looking for additional leads and possibly even trying to corroborate from foundry records. At this date and time, I will conjecture that it is very likely the bell from the Methodist church in Old Cahawba. Should future evidence say otherwise, then that is indeed all the greater for the sake of authenticating history. Historians often see things dimly and can only make hypotheses in identifying and placing people, events and things in the framework of

Right: The old Methodist church in Cahawba, where the Maplesville Baptist bell is believed to have come from. *From the Alabama Department of Archives and History.*

Below: Maplesville Baptist Church today. *From Clem Clapp.*

The 1859 Meneely West Troy bell in the church steeple. *From the author.*

the historical narrative. It only seems right to believe that the Maplesville Baptist Church bell, in its earlier life, very likely towered above the Civil War events at Old Cahawba, including Union general Emory Upton's meeting with Confederate general Nathan Bedford Forrest under a flag of truce to discuss the exchange of prisoners on April 6, 1865, and most certainly by the prisoners at the Confederate prison known as Castle Morgan, and it remains with us even today, causing us to pause and reflect on this important period of Alabama, Civil War and United States history.

17
ABBEVILLE METHODIST CHURCH

SURVIVED UNION GENERAL GRIERSON'S APRIL 1865 CAMPAIGN TO EUFAULA

*T*he drive from Montgomery to Abbeville, in Henry County, Alabama, is one of the most beautiful and scenic drives in the state. After turning onto Highway 10 in Brundidge, the entire landscape just seems to open up under a big sky of huge cumulonimbus clouds, and there are stretches of green, open prairie as far as the eye can see. At the end of the journey is the beautiful hamlet of Abbeville, a town where time seems to stand still, yet it is bustling with life. Here, one senses the oldness of the land and how roots grow deeper; life is sweeter; and faith, love and neighborliness abound in a city and county older than the state of Alabama. It is a city that played a significant role in the Civil War, and it is where Rosa Parks also lived for a time.

In the heart of Abbeville, at the intersection of Doswell and Kelly Streets, is Abbeville United Methodist Church, an interesting architectural expression of Gothic with Romanesque accents. It was designed and built by local architect and builder Zachariah T. Kirkland, who also designed the 1889 Henry County Courthouse, which is now demolished. Zachariah T. Kirkland was also ably assisted in the construction effort by Allen A. Kirkland, Irvin Kirkland and Edward Crawford, who is credited with placing the cross atop the steeple.

The Methodist Church came to Henry County prior to 1825 as part of the Lawrenceville Circuit, and the church in Abbeville was organized in either 1830 or 1850, as accounts of the church's founding differ in narrative. The first church building was a wooden two-story building located on East Washington Street. It housed the Masonic lodge on the second floor and

Abbeville United Methodist Church. *From Garrett Law.*

obviously had a belfry, as the historical account refers to the church's present bell as the "original bell." In 1894, work began on the second, and present, church sanctuary on the lot known as the "wagon yard," where wagons parked when they came to town and where horses and mules were refreshed. The church was completed in 1896 and has been a shining star for Abbeville and Alabama as a great example of architecture, with the beautiful stained-glass windows inside the sanctuary, one of which honors the soldiers of World War I.

The Abbeville United Methodist Church bell was very likely procured after the congregation began worshiping in the first church building on East Washington Street, since it was cast in 1859 by the Meneely West Troy Bell Foundry of Troy, New York. Though the bell is not large, the cost of buying it—for a small or medium congregation—was high. A benefactor may have donated it, for that matter. This speaks to a quality found in the congregation of desiring the church to be respectful, reverent and ecclesiastical to the community by ringing the bell to summon worshipers. It was also used for other purposes—even as a fire alarm, as church bells doubled to sound the alarm when fire broke out. Cast before the Civil War,

Historic Alabama Bells

Above, left: The 1859 Meneely West Troy church bell in the tower of the Abbeville United Methodist Church. *From Garrett Law.*

Above, right: Believed to be by Tiffany, the stained-glass window "Soldier and Angel," in memory of William S. Parker, a World War I soldier. *From Garrett Law.*

Left: The Abbeville church bell in its mountings high in the church tower. The bell appears to have its original hardware and mountings. *From Garrett Law.*

Top: The bell founder's inscription on the Abbeville bell. *From Garrett Law.*

Left: The inscription of the date of casting. Notice the typeface used. *From Garrett Law.*

when the clouds of war were not yet gathering so ominously, it was a nice addition to the church and added another dimension of beauty and grace to the church as it could be heard for miles around, summoning worshipers to church.

When the Union was divided and the Civil War erupted, it was quite amazing that the Abbeville church bell remained intact in the tower and was not melted down to make ordnance for the Confederacy. However, as the war continued, the threat of being melted never went away, and even after

Lee surrendered to Grant at Appomattox on April 9, 1865, Union forces continued carrying out orders from Grant to destroy all of the Confederate ammunitions and manufacturing plants. Were bells still at risk during this time? One could answer no, but this would be an inconclusive answer. Until all of the fighting stopped, everything was under threat, including the church bell at Abbeville.

When Union general Benjamin H. Grierson made his way to Eufaula on April 29, 1865, coming within miles of Abbeville, it seemed very likely that the entire town would be under a potential threat, but Abbeville survived, and the Methodist Meneely West Troy church bell with it. Today, the Abbeville church bell hangs in the church tower untouched and unscathed, calling worshipers to service now, as it did then, with its beautiful sweet peal heard for miles around in this loveliest of pastoral settings.

18
FIRST BAPTIST CHURCH, RIPLEY

The Bell that Watched Over the Freedom Riders

Organized in 1866 by parishioners who had worshiped at the First Baptist Church in Montgomery, the First Baptist Church on North Ripley Street, also known as the Columbus Street Baptist Church, was created as one of the first African American churches in the Montgomery area. The congregation met in a wooden building on the corner of Columbus and Ripley Streets until fire destroyed the wood structure. Following the tragic event, Pastor Andrew Jackson Stokes led a campaign to rebuild the church from 1910 to 1915 and retained architect Walter T. Bailey, a professor at Tuskegee Institute, as it was known then, to design the new sanctuary. Bailey did so in a marvelous indigenous expression of French Romanesque true to the polychromatic tone and texture of the style and rendered in brick and stone. Likely inspired by Bailey's beautiful design, as well as good old-fashioned budget limitations, church members were encouraged to find and bring a brick a day to the construction site. This led to the church's alternate name: the Brick-A-Day Church.

The church bell was cast by Clinton H. Meneely Bell Foundry of Troy, New York, in 1910. The bell is beautifully cast with a colorful patina and is inscribed with the names of honored leaders from the Brick-A-Day Church:

Peace On Earth and Good Will To All Men
Deacon Alex Hamlin, Deacon Ned Casby, Deacon King Hatcher
Deacon Henry Vaughn, Deacon George Haskin, Deacon Alfred Dotson
Deacon Russell Johnson, Deacon Henry Speare, Deacon Mace Coleman
Horace S. Martin, Clerk
Organized 1866 Rev. Andrew Jackson Stokes D.D., L.L.D., 1911
Pastor

The First Baptist Church, known as the Brick-A-Day Church, designed by architect W.T. Bailey of Tuskegee Institute, as it was known then. *From the author.*

The foundry inscription is different than other bells by Clinton H. Meneely. It simply states:

Meneely Bell Company
Troy, N.Y.
1910

These bells would typically be inscribed with "Clinton H. Meneely Bell Company Troy, N.Y., U.S.A.," followed by the year.

Among the ranks of churches that were active participants in the civil rights movement, especially under the pastorate and leadership of Reverend Ralph D. Abernathy from 1952 to 1961, First Baptist Church on Ripley has suffered greatly. In 1957, both the church and its parsonage were bombed,

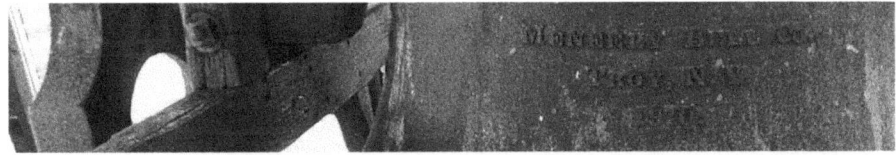

This page, top: Inscription bearing the name of the bell foundry and the casting date. *From the author.*

This page, bottom: The A-mounts, or A-stands, of the church bell. *From the author.*

Opposite, top: The church bell visible from the street in the tower of the First Baptist Church. *From the author.*

Opposite, bottom: The First Baptist Church bell cast by the Meneely Bell Company in 1910. It is mounted in the belfry with its original hardware and mountings. *From the author.*

which no doubt led to the first Institute on Nonviolence and Social Change during the very same year. This was convened at the church and sponsored by the Southern Christian Leadership Conference. In 1961, the Freedom Riders, who were savagely attacked at the Greyhound Station in downtown Montgomery, found refuge at the church along with church members and others but were trapped inside by a large and violent mob. U.S. attorney

Inscription invoking the latter part of Luke 2:14 and honoring the church's leaders from that era of the church's history. *From the author.*

The bell's tolling striker, or hammer. *From the author.*

View of the top of the bell tower in admiration of architect Walter T. Bailey's historical revivalist touches. *From the author.*

The design intrigue of the lower tower—an expression of affection for the French Romanesque—in full architectural bloom here by Bailey. *From the author.*

general Robert F. Kennedy federalized the Alabama National Guard to give them safe passage from the church more than fourteen hours later. Among the brave and courageous Freedom Riders who were given safe conduct from the violent mob was a young John Robert Lewis from Troy, Alabama, who later became, and is at the time of this writing, a highly respected and long-serving congressman from Georgia's fifth congressional district.

The bell, high in the tower of this beautiful church, was witness to all of the tragic events of the church's history. But it also watched over the brave Freedom Riders and the birth of one of the greatest movements in our nation, and the world, for liberty, freedom and equality.

19
MOUNT ZION AME ZION CHURCH

THE TOWER BELL COMES HOME FOR CIVIL RIGHTS HISTORY

*M*ount Zion AME Zion Church is where, after the arrest of Rosa Parks, Reverend Roy Bennett met with community leaders to begin organizing the Montgomery Improvement Association (MIA). Formed in December 1955, the members elected a young, and rather reluctant, Dr. Martin Luther King Jr. at the MIA's first meeting. The MIA became the organizing force behind the 1955–56 Montgomery Bus Boycott, which ended segregated seating on Montgomery's city buses and established a significant beachhead in the civil rights movement. One could say that this church is where people began to come together, in unity of spirit and purpose, to improve the lives of Montgomery's African American community. Because of the events that happened here, and because the church was where Dr. King rose to the forefront of the historic struggle for civil rights, Mount Zion AME Zion Church is highly significant as a historic national landmark.

The church was constructed in 1899 and renovated to its present architectural appearance in 1921. The church is astoundingly proportional in its façade configuration, strongly suggesting the possibility of Jim Alexander as the architect, according to Charles P. Everett, a member of the Mount Zion AME Zion Church and leader in the quest to transform the historic church into a museum. Everett also maintains that the church bears a strikingly similar appearance to the Old Ship of Zion church, which Alexander is reported to have designed. Indeed, it does, as it is proportionally correct—something the Italian great Andreo Palladio would be proud of if he were in our time and place.

Right: Mount Zion AME Zion Church on Holt Street. *From the author.*

Below: The original cast steel alloy church bell being taken down from the new Mount Zion AME Zion Church. *From Charles P. Everett, Mount Zion AME Zion Church.*

Historic Alabama Bells

Top: Lifting the bell for loading and transport to the historic Mount Zion AME Zion Church. *From Charles P. Everett, Mount Zion AME Zion Church.*

Bottom: Loading the bell for the journey to its original residence. *From Charles P. Everett, Mount Zion AME Zion Church.*

When the church built a new sanctuary in 1990, the bell, a steel alloy casting that weighs around 350 pounds, was taken down from the church tower and moved to the new church, where it remained for several years. However, since the emergence of a recent initiative to transform the old historic church into a museum, the bell was once again moved and placed back in the church tower. This historic bell actually rang for the marchers who walked past the church on the fiftieth anniversary of the Selma to Montgomery marches, and it will continue to ring on those historic and eventful occasions as a great symbol of the civil rights movement.

OLD SHIP AME ZION CHURCH

Pulling Hard on the Rope

Organized around 1850 as a church plant by the Court Street Methodist Church, the newly formed black congregation was offered the sponsoring church's 1835 wooden sanctuary if it would move it to a different location, which it did, transporting it on log rollers to its current location at the corner of Holcombe and Mildred Streets. Legend says that a local bystander who observed the church being moved by the men on the log rollers shouted, "What do you have there?"

One of the crew replied, "It is the Old Ship of Zion, moving on." Reaching the new church site, the crew placed the wooden church on piers to accommodate the change in elevation. This original wooden structure was altered in the 1850s and was bricked up around 1888. The most significant change to the structure occurred from 1918 to 1920, when it was transformed into an expression of Classical Revivalism by architect Jim Alexander. We know very little about Alexander, but he was obviously a designer with Georgian and Palladian aspirations. The façade is truly one of the most beautiful and proportional in Montgomery and beyond. The diagrams of the Golden Section are apparent to any architect beholding the church's frontispiece.

Old Ship AME Zion Church is rich with history, as we have seen already just by virtue of its architecture. The church was also the site of many important and critical meetings for the civil rights movement. It has also been the host of speeches by not only Dr. Martin Luther King Jr. during the civil rights movement but also Frederick Douglass, Governor Thomas Kilby,

Old Ship of Zion AME Church. The major renovation and front facade were designed by architect Jim Alexander and is proportionally perfect to the Golden Section. *From the author.*

The access ladder on the top landing that leads to the Old Ship Church's belfry. *From the author.*

Old Ship's bell, cast in 1876 by the Buckeye Bell Foundry, also known as the Vanduzen Tift Bell Foundry, of Cincinnati, Ohio. *From the author.*

Booker T. Washington and President William McKinley. In the belfry of the southern tower, the church has a very special bronze bell cast by the Buckeye Bell Foundry, also known as the Vanduzen Tift Foundry of Cincinnati, Ohio, cast in the year of the United States' centennial—1876. These bells are almost always identified by the two bolts visible at the top of the bell yoke. Although the church's history as Montgomery's oldest black congregation dates back to 1850, how and when the bell came into the possession of the church remains unknown. It is a very fine bell with a beautiful peal, blessing all who hear its wonderful sound in the capital city.

21

BROWN CHAPEL AME CHURCH, SELMA

The Bell that Began the March for Civil Rights

       The ancestral roots of Brown Chapel AME Church, one of the most visible symbols of the civil rights movement, go back to the time when freed slaves began worshiping at the First Methodist Episcopal Church South in Selma. Upon the passage of the Emancipation Proclamation, the freed slaves started meeting in the basement of the Albert Hotel, enjoying the new measure of autonomy in their faith by having their own church, or the early origins of it. The AME church was known for outreach to slaves during the Civil War, and in the postwar years, these congregations continued to share the Gospel. The Albert Hotel congregation, which was known as the Colored AME Church of the South, was one such example and was a Sunday school when it began. In 1867, the church congregation applied for membership in the African Methodist Episcopal Church and was received into the convention. Under the shepherding of Bishop John Mifflin Brown, it was named Brown Chapel AME Church. A year later, the first Alabama conference of the AME church was organized at Brown Chapel, and in 1869, the first building was erected on the current site. Several years later, the current, and beautifully designed, sanctuary was built. It is an amazing expression of architectural Eclecticism.

    Designed and built by architect A.J. Farley, Brown Chapel AME Church is at once an impression of something Georgian, Romanesque, Mission, Federal and Eclectic, due to the Oriental hints and early American treatments. It's an amazing building. The church's design has what my former professor of architecture, Muir Stewart of Auburn University, called "real architectural

Left; Brown Chapel AME Church, designed by architect A.J. Farley in 1908. This is the church where the civil rights march began in 1965. *From the author.*

Below: Rear view of the Brown Chapel bell cast in 1881 by the McShane Bell Foundry in Baltimore, Maryland. *From the author.*

Historic Alabama Bells

Upshot of the large McShane bell with the tolling striker. *From the author.*

power," otherwise translated as "Gestalt," because people identify with and understand it. And there is even a Postmodern feel to the design. Brown Chapel is a real architectural treasure.

Within the belfry of the north tower is another treasure that is so very meaningful and invaluable to the church: the 1881 McShane bell cast by the McShane Bell Foundry of Baltimore, Maryland. The approximately thirty-six-inch-diameter bell has aged with a beautiful patina and weighs around one thousand pounds.

Reverend Leodis Strong, pastor of Brown Chapel AME Church, was keenly interested to find the answer to my question of whether the bell rang during the courageous and heroic Selma to Montgomery march for civil rights in 1965.

Pastor Strong immediately recalled that longtime parishioner Joyce Parrish O'Neal was a church member at the time and participated in the march. He telephoned her to ask whether the bell rang on the day of the march, and she clearly remembered that it did! The bell was rung by the church sexton, Mr. Edward Davis, on a regular basis during the month between Sunday school and worship, and it did in fact ring before the

Historic Alabama Bells

Above: The front side of the Brown Chapel bell with the bell founder's inscription and date of casting. *From the author.*

Left: View of the bell as you climb into the tower belfry. *From the author.*

march on Bloody Sunday! This revelation confirmed a portion of the civil rights history never before known. Now thanks to Reverend Strong and Ms. O'Neal, we know about the bell's connection to the history of the civil rights march, which adds another element to the significance of Brown Chapel being the starting point for the march from Selma to Montgomery. In the future, we may know more about how the church obtained this beautiful bell, but at present, very little is known about its history with the church. But no matter, what is known is what is most important—civil rights for every United States citizen.

22
SIXTEENTH STREET BAPTIST CHURCH

Tolling for a National Tragedy

*A*s the site of one of the darkest moments of our nation, the Sixteenth Street Baptist Church has also come to symbolize the conscience of the United States for civil rights. September 15, 1963, was forever engraved on the hearts of Americans as a reminder of the evil and consequences of racism when Addie Mae Collins, Denise McNair, Carole Robertson and Cynthia Wesley were tragically killed in a hate bombing by the Ku Klux Klan before the morning worship service.

The aftermath of this shocking and tragic event deeply affected our country, jolting citizens to the reality of the effects of racism and arousing widespread concern and action for the cause of civil rights. This tragedy, followed by the assassination of President John F. Kennedy on November 22, 1963, put the nation into a deep sense of grieving, mourning and outrage. The following year, the Civil Rights Act of 1964 was passed and signed into law by President Lyndon B. Johnson. It was enacted because of the tragedy of Sixteenth Street and because of the assassination of President Kennedy, who was a positive force for civil rights in his presidency.

As a silent witness to untold grief, tragedy and pain, the bell and the tower of the Sixteenth Street Baptist Church felt the impact of the blast that morning. The bell was cast by the National Bell Foundry of Cincinnati, Ohio, and the date of casting is unknown at the time of this writing. The hands who made this bell would be so amazed to learn how significant their creation would become one day as a symbol of memory and hope for the cause of civil rights in the United States and worldwide. On August 28, 2013,

Sixteenth Street Baptist Church, which was designed by architect Wallace Rayfield, as photographed by Birmingham photographer O.V. Hunt in 1924. *From Birmingham Public Library Archives.*

Aftermath of the September 15, 1963 church bombing that killed Addie Mae Collins, Cynthia Wesley, Carole Robertson and Denise McNair. *From Alabama Department of Archives and History.*

Historic Alabama Bells

The steel alloy bell of the Sixteenth Street Baptist Church, which was cast by the National Bell Company of Cincinnati, Ohio. *From WBRC TV6.*

President Barack Obama and the Sixteenth Street Baptist Church bell at the fiftieth anniversary of the March on Washington in 2013. *From Getty Images.*

the Sixteenth Street Baptist Church bell was the centerpiece of the fiftieth anniversary of Dr. Martin Luther King Jr.'s "I Have a Dream" speech on the steps of the Lincoln Memorial in our nation's capital. It was struck fifty times in commemoration of each year since Dr. King's stirring and awe-inspiring speech and was hosted by President Barack Obama and civil rights leaders and dignitaries.

Sixteenth Street Baptist Church was designed in 1911 by African American architect Wallace Augustus Rayfield in an architectural expression reminiscent of Romanesque and Mannerism with some vestigial traces of the Adriatic in the scheme. One could almost say that Rayfield was, in a sense, experimenting with what would later come to be known as Postmodernism. Based on other work by the hand of Rayfield, this is certainly very plausible from a man who was educated at Howard University, the Pratt Institute and Columbia University and who later became the director of the Architectural and Mechanical Drawing Department at Tuskegee Institute.

Rayfield's time was during the historical revivalist movement in architecture in the United States. He was reinforced by training in the manner of the École des Beaux-Arts School movement, which was the deep-rooted standard for formal architectural education and professional practice for the American architect until the advent of modernism, which he also had exposure to. His essay for Sixteenth Street Baptist was the ideal expression for what would later become such an important historic landmark through tragedy. But the sweet peal of the bell within the Rayfield-designed tower indeed brings hope and healing to all for the cause of civil rights in our country.

23
EVER RINGING THE BELLS OF FREEDOM

A Bell for Every Historic Civil Rights Church

*I*n doing research for this book, I tended to presuppose that wherever there was a tower, steeple, cupola or bell cote, there would be a bell within. Nearly all the time there was, but sometimes there was not! This was surprising to me in a number of instances, due to the fact that there were incredibly tall and beautiful towers with louvered openings on all sides of the towers, but no bells!

When I was exploring and investigating three historical, critically important and highly significant churches of the civil rights movement, I was either told or knew firsthand that there were no bells in the towers of those churches, all located in Montgomery, namely Dexter King Memorial Baptist Church on Dexter Avenue, Holt Street Baptist Church and the City of Saint Jude Catholic Church on Fairview Avenue.

Dexter King Memorial Baptist Church was the pastorate of Dr. Martin Luther King Jr. while he was leading the civil rights movement in the '50s. The church was host to the mass meetings that led to the planning of the Montgomery Bus Boycott and is an example of a historic civil rights church that might not have a bell in the steeple. In searching for clues to support the claim, it was necessary to inquire from the church itself and make observations from the interior of the church, which revealed that there is no wall ladder, no evidence of a hole in the ceiling for a rope and no rope! Nonetheless, how wonderful it would be if the church could confirm a bell honoring Dr. King and others, if so desired. This would be a very meaningful and worthwhile endeavor and would help pass the torch of Dr. King's legacy and civil rights. I hope this idea would be very earnestly considered.

Historic Alabama Bells

Left: An 1870 Jones and Company Catalog illustration for hoisting a bell into a tower. *From public domain.*

Right: Dexter King Memorial Baptist Church in Montgomery. *From the author.*

Holt Street Baptist Church is where Dr. King gave his passionate, courageous and rousing speech championing action with nonviolence. This led to the Montgomery Bus Boycott of 1955 and 1956, which protested the City of Montgomery's segregated seating ordinance on buses after Rosa Parks was arrested for refusing to give up her seat "for whites only." The church is a beautiful example of Mid-Century Gothic and has a tower on the side of the sanctuary near the rear of the church. My research findings conclude that there is not, and likely never was, a bell in the tower, based on telephone interviews and even firsthand observation from the street. Holt Street is currently undergoing an extensive restoration and will become a museum. To begin a campaign to cast and install a bell honoring the church's role in the civil rights history would only add to the magnificence of the awesome spirit and dedication in this present endeavor.

Holt Street Baptist Church belfry. *From the author.*

Holt Street Baptist Church. *From the author.*

City of Saint Jude Catholic Church, the site of the final camp before marching to the capitol steps. *From the author.*

The City of Saint Jude Catholic Church was the site of the last camp before the last leg of the march for civil rights into and through downtown Montgomery, concluding on the steps of the Alabama State Capitol. I knew about the tower of the City of Saint Jude from when, as a new resident to Montgomery thirty years ago, I began venturing out to see the sights and came across this beautiful early Christian basilica. One day, I ventured inside and climbed the balcony to see where the access to the tower was. I really wasn't going to climb but wondered how one got up there. Just then, the priest was walking in the sanctuary and spotted me. He asked if he could help me. I replied how fascinated I was with the church and that I worked in architecture and was curious about the tower if it had a bell.

To my surprise, he pointed me to the access and gave me permission to go up. What a dream come true! I made my way to the access and began climbing up more than one ladder. When I finally got to the top, I was expecting to see at least one large bell, or maybe chimes, but I did not. The church was designed for not only one bell but several it seemed. It would be a great initiative to realize a bell, or several, for the City of Saint Jude to use during worship and to honor the history of the civil rights movement. It is my sincere hope that these ideas may receive earnest consideration with real bells, not the electronic versions. This is only fitting, as two centuries from now, the bell will survive as an archival artifact, whereas electronic systems seem to have a limited life span by comparison.

While researching, I tried to offer the courtesy of calling before coming, especially try to find out if there truly was an object of substance in the tower. Some people I called on did not know and had to check. Others seemed resolute that there was nothing there. Sometimes they were wrong. In seeking confirmation of evidence, it is possible that I may be proven wrong. But I can assure you that I have checked the information as thoroughly as I can while not being able to climb up into the forbidden-access belfries to find out what is up there. I am totally relying on information from those who have been there or have been longtime members of the church and did not believe that one was there.

For the churches presented here that do not have, or have never had, a bell, there is no shame at all in not possessing one. A number of churches with steeples and towers do not have bells! I'm thinking even now of a large and grand church in our state that I have loved since I was a child, and its tower could hold a carillon and even a bell at the very top! One day I called the church to inquire, and the minister shared with me that the church never has had a bell since it was built in the '20s.

Detail of the City of Saint Jude bell tower. *From the author.*

In my view, no church anywhere—historic or not—should ever feel badly about not having a bell, even over a lengthy period of time. The best way to view such a situation is to see it as an opportunity to do something special for a church's future. It could be a way of commemorating or honoring someone or a group of individuals in a special way. Churches that have bells that are not safe to ring have the same opportunity by restoring their bells to service and dedicating the bells to those special people deemed to be so honored.

It is my hope that the readers of this book may rediscover the wonder, beauty and glorious sound of bells—not electronic pseudo-bells or chimes, but the genuine article, something that a church or institution can take pride in, which has value and meaning and actually brings people together in every way. This would be so true for Alabama's plethora of historic churches, but actually, this idea is meant to be for all—all who love bells and want to rediscover their church or tower bell and the joy of ringing it for all to hear and be touched by their unique sound and tone.

May these, and all bells, ever ring from every steeple, dome, clock tower and cupola, both now and always, as Providence hath so decreed. May it be so, dear reader.

BIBLIOGRAPHY

Abbott, Edward. *The Bell's Own Story*. N.p.: Books on Demand. First published 1901 by Press of Powell and Company (Cambridge, MA).

Dzeda, Joe. "Ithiel Town, Architect of Trinity Church." Trinity Church on the Green. 2008. http://trinitynewhaven.org.

Eckhardt, George H. *Pennsylvania Clocks and Clockmakers*. New York: Bonanza, 1955.

French, Thomas L., Jr., and Edward L. French. "Horace King, Bridge Builder." *Alabama Heritage* 11 (Winter 1989).

Goeppinger, Neil. *Large Bells of America*. Sarasota, FL: Suncoast Digital Press, 2016.

Hughes, Delos. *Historic Alabama Courthouses*. Montgomery, AL: NewSouth Books, 2017.

Neeley, Mary Ann. *The Works of Matthew Blue: Montgomery's First Historian*. Montgomery, AL: NewSouth Books, 2010.

Renton, Herbert S. "In Early Days—XXI." *Domestic Engineering: An Illustrated Weekly* 47, no. 10 (June 5, 1909): 297–98.

Ross, Sydney. *The Bell Casters of Troy*. Troy, NY: Hudson Mohawk Industrial Gateway, 2002.

Shelley, Frederick. *Early American Tower Clocks: Surviving American Tower Clocks from 1720 to 1870, with Profiles of All Known American Makers*. Columbia, PA: National Association of Watch Clock Collectors, 1999.

Springer, L. Elsinore. *That Vanishing Sound*. New York: Crown Publishers, 1976.

Stickney, Edward, and Evelyn Stickney. *The Bells of Paul Revere, His Sons, and His Grandsons*. Bedford, MA, 1976.

ABOUT THE AUTHOR

*T*homas Kaufmann is an architectural historian, preservationist and artist who studied architecture at Auburn University and the Institute of Classical Architecture and Art in New York, where he serves as a Fellow Emeritus. He and his wife, Ann Marie, and their son, Tommy, live in a 1926 Craftsman bungalow in the historic Capitol Heights neighborhood of Montgomery, Alabama.

www.ingramcontent.com/pod-product-compliance
Lightning Source LLC
Chambersburg PA
CBHW040251170426
43191CB00018B/2374